MW01268116

THE HONEST MAN'S FORTUNE

THE MALONE SOCIETY
REPRINTS VOL. 176
2009 (2012)

PUBLISHED FOR THE MALONE SOCIETY
BY MANCHESTER UNIVERSITY PRESS

Oxford Road, Manchester M13 9NR, UK
and Room 400, 175 Fifth Avenue, New York, NY 10010, USA
www.manchesteruniversitypress.co.uk

Distributed exclusively in the USA by
Palgrave, 175 Fifth Avenue, New York,
NY 10010, USA

Distributed exclusively in Canada by
UBC Press, University of British Columbia, 2029 West Mall,
Vancouver, BC, Canada V6T 1Z2

British Library Cataloguing-in-Publication Data
A catalogue record for this book is available from the British Library

Library of Congress Cataloging-in-Publication Data applied for

ISBN 978–0–7190–8611–3

Typeset by New Leaf Design, Scarborough, North Yorkshire

Printed by Henry Ling Limited, at the Dorset Press, Dorchester, DT1 1HD

This edition of *The Honest Man's Fortune* was prepared by Grace Ioppolo, and checked by H. R. Woudhuysen and G. R. Proudfoot. The Society is grateful to the National Art Library of the Victoria and Albert Museum for permission to publish the play, from the unique manuscript (Dyce MS 9), and to reproduce pages from it.

February 2011 H. R. WOUDHUYSEN

INTRODUCTION

The Honest Man's Fortune is preserved in a manuscript text (Victoria and Albert Museum, Dyce MS 9, shelfmark Dyce 25.F.9) and in a printed text in the 1647 Folio of the works of Francis Beaumont and John Fletcher, titled *Comedies and Tragedies ... Never Printed Before, and Now Published By the Authours Originall Copies*, printed for Humphrey Robinson and Humphrey Moseley. The Folio text (F1) was reprinted in subsequent collected editions of Beaumont and Fletcher's works in 1679, 1711, 1750, 1778, 1811, 1812, and 1840. In 1843, the Reverend Alexander Dyce, who purchased the manuscript of the play and later donated it to what became the Victoria and Albert Museum, published an edition of the play based on a collation of the manuscript and F1 in the third of the eleven volumes of his edition of *The Works of Beaumont and Fletcher* (1843–6). Although the manuscript and F1 texts of the play may have been copied from the same manuscript, they differ substantively, as the F1 text contains one extra scene (5.3) and an expanded concluding scene (5.4).

There are two modern scholarly editions of the play: Johan Gerritsen's was based largely on the manuscript, Cyrus Hoy's on F1.[1] The aim of this edition is to produce, for the first time, a text of the manuscript, which is now in a very fragile state.

The Manuscript: Provenance

The manuscript of *The Honest Man's Fortune* is among a collection of dramatic manuscripts including *The Faithful Friends*, *The Parliament of Love*, and *Timon* acquired by Dyce (1798–1869), a scholar and editor not only of the plays of Beaumont and Fletcher, but of Marlowe, Middleton, Shakespeare, Webster, and other sixteenth- and seventeenth-century dramatists. On 18 February 1836, the bookseller Thomas Rodd, the younger (1796–1849), purchased the manuscript of *The Honest Man's Fortune* evidently for Dyce at Sotheby's sale of manuscripts from Richard Heber's library.[2] At his death, Dyce bequeathed this and the other play manuscripts to the South Kensington Museum, the former name of the Victoria and Albert Museum, where they remain among the collections of the National Art Library.

As to its provenance before the Heber sale, if this manuscript was not made for the play's original owners, the Lady Elizabeth's Men, it was made for the play's next owners, the King's Men. At least this or some other manuscript of the play stayed in their repertory, for on 7 August 1641 *The Honest Man's Fortune* was listed among thirty plays that the King's Men

[1] *The Honest Mans Fortune: A Critical Edition of MS Dyce 9 (1625)*, ed. Johan Gerritsen (Groningen and Djakarta, 1952); *The Honest Man's Fortune*, ed. Cyrus Hoy, in *The Dramatic Works in the Beaumont and Fletcher Canon*, gen. ed. Fredson Bowers, 10 vols. (Cambridge, 1966–96), x. 1–144.

[2] *Bibliotheca Heberiana, Part the Eleventh*, item 1322. Gerritsen, p. xviii, notes that annotated copies of the sale catalogue show the price realised was 4*s*. and that Dyce paid 16*s*. for it.

did not want printed.[3] On 4 September 1646 the play was entered in the Stationers' Register by Humphrey Robinson and Humphrey Moseley, who published it in the Beaumont and Fletcher Folio in 1647.[4] As the manuscript lacks marks for casting off the copy and contains substantive variants from the text of the play in F1, it was not used as printer's copy for this first printed edition of the play. At the reopening of the theatres in 1660, some companies were re-formed, and they revived plays in their repertory. *The Honest Man's Fortune* is first mentioned on 20 August 1668, when the play, and possibly this manuscript, was assigned by royal patent to the Duke's Company, managed by William Davenant. The company amalgamated in 1682 with the King's Company, managed by Thomas Killigrew, to produce the United Company.[5] Thus the rights to the play, and any company 'book', that is, prompt-book, of it, would have passed to this later company. Malone noted in his essay 'An Historical Account of the English Stage', published in his 1790 edition of the works of Shakespeare, that he had in his possession a manuscript of *The Honest Man's Fortune* dated 1613.[6]

That Malone and the Duke's Company were in possession of the same manuscript of the play, almost certainly this one, can be conjectured on the basis of one strong connection between them: the private library of William Cartwright, the younger (1606–86), a Caroline and Restoration actor, bookseller, and bibliophile. Cartwright was the son of the actor William Cartwright, who had himself been a colleague and business partner of the prominent tragedian and theatrical entrepreneur Edward Alleyn. The younger Cartwright was a sharer in the King's Company and remained in it until its re-formation in 1682 as the United Company. At his death, the younger Cartwright bequeathed one hundred play manuscripts, in addition to books and actors' portraits, to Dulwich College in order to form a theatrical library in honour of Alleyn, its founder.[7] Today Dulwich College

[3] G. E. Bentley, *The Jacobean and Caroline Stage*, 7 vols. (Oxford, 1941–69), i. 65–6.

[4] W. W. Greg, *A Bibliography of the English Printed Drama to the Restoration*, 4 vols. (London, 1939–59), i. 56–7. For discussions of the printing of the Folio text of the play, including arguments that the same manuscript was used as printer's copy for F1 and in the copying of the Dyce manuscript, see Gerritsen, pp. xxxv–lxviii and Hoy, Textual Introduction, 4–14. Hoy established that the play's printer was Edward Griffin.

[5] Allardyce Nicoll, *A History of Restoration Drama, 1660–1700*, 2nd edn. (Cambridge, 1928), p. 315.

[6] 'An Historical Account of the English Stage', in *The Plays and Poems of William Shakespeare*, ed. Edmond Malone, 10 vols. (London, 1790), Vol. 1, Part 2, pp. 223, 226. Malone states, 'The manuscript copy of the *Honest Man's Fortune* is now before me, and is dated 1613. It was therefore probably the joint production of Beaumont and Fletcher. This piece was acted at the Globe, and the copy which had been licensed by Sir George Buc, was without doubt destroyed by the fire which consumed that theatre in the year 1613' (p. 226). However, there is no evidence that this play was the property of the King's Men at the time of the Globe fire, and modern attribution studies do not include Beaumont as an author of the play. See the section on Authorship below, pp. xix–xxi.

[7] See Cartwright's will in *Playhouse Wills, 1558–1642: An Edition of Wills by Shakespeare and His Contemporaries in the London Theatre*, ed. E. A. J. Honigmann and Susan Brock (Manchester, 1993), pp. 238–44.

possesses only one play manuscript, of *The Telltale*, which was wrapped up with the theatrical plot of *The Seven Deadly Sins, Part 2*, reclaimed by the College from an 1825 auction of books of James Boswell the younger, Malone's literary executor. In fact, Malone had borrowed numerous manuscripts from the College and, according to John Payne Collier, had sometimes failed to return them.[8] As College records show, Malone kept the manuscript of Henslowe's famous Diary for a number of years before the College demanded its return.

The Dyce manuscript of *The Honest Man's Fortune*, a play most likely commissioned by Henslowe, who shared his theatrical profits with his son-in-law Alleyn, could have been acquired by Cartwright from the United Company and bequeathed in 1685 with his other play manuscripts to Dulwich College. Malone may have removed this manuscript from the College, possibly returning it at a later point. Auction catalogues before the Heber sale do not list the manuscript of *The Honest Man's Fortune*, nor is there any other information to determine how it was acquired by Heber. It is possible that it came into his possession at some point directly from Malone's library, or from a private dealer, or from one of the other collectors, including John Payne Collier, who had removed documents from the College's archive prior to 1836.

Physical Description

The manuscript is made up of a single loose leaf, which has the title on the recto (see Plate 1) and a blank verso, and seventeen sheets, each folded into a bifolium, giving a total of thirty-five folios. The leaves measure 320 mm × 220 mm, with some later leaves being very slightly smaller in size. The conjugate sheets suggest that the scribe worked with one folded sheet at a time before they were sewn together, rather than writing on quired sheets or in an already made-up and bound book. In writing on successive bifolia, he followed a pattern that appears to have been common for authors and scribes producing play manuscripts.[9]

The manuscript was rebound in the nineteenth century, most likely for Dyce, with the title leaf and each bifolium interleaved with a sheet of modern paper. The extremely fragile condition of the manuscript, with some small loss of paper following each attempt to turn a page, precludes close investigation of the watermarks and of the now damaged binding, but a cursory examination concurs with Gerritsen's findings in his edition. First, the binding is 'half-russia with marbled boards and russia tips, tooled and

[8] *The Alleyn Papers: A Collection of Original Documents Illustrative of the Life and Times of Edward Alleyn, and of the Early English Stage and Drama*, ed. John Payne Collier, Shakespeare Society Publications 18 (1843), pp. v–vi.

[9] See Grace Ioppolo, *Dramatists and their Manuscripts in the Age of Shakespeare, Jonson, Middleton and Heywood: Authorship, Authority and the Playhouse* (London, 2006), pp. 87–8.

the spine lettered in gold' with the play's title.[10] Secondly, in addition to the interleaved modern paper, the manuscript uses a mixed stock of paper (with only one unwatermarked leaf, used for the title-page), showing six distinct watermarks. The first two are different croziers (similar to Heawood numbers 1216–18), with the first crozier in Fols. 1, 5, 7, 11, 14, and 15, and the second in Fols. 4 and 10. The second are two separate post or pillar watermarks (similar to Heawood numbers 3499–502), with the first in Fol. 17, and the second in Fols. 24, 26, 27, 30, 31, and 33. The final two are different pot watermarks (similar to Heawood numbers 3583–7), with the first in Fol. 20 and the second in Fol. 22.[11]

The paper has suffered damage, particularly in the upper corners of the leaves' outer edges where some of the original foliation has been lost. Gerritsen notes that 'Some leaves of the original MS have been trimmed with the shears, presumably in binding, in order to prevent incipient tears from going farther.'[12] Further damage along the foot of the manuscript's pages has, on occasion, caused the loss of letters or words in speech prefixes, dialogue, or stage directions, including the loss of a stage direction and most of the speech prefix at TLN 2623 on Fol. 31a and of an actor's name from the licence on the final page.

All the characteristics of the layout, as well as the numerous marks for cuts, suggest that the manuscript served as a company 'book', the contemporary term for a prompt-book, from which actors' parts were copied and from which the 'book-keeper' kept track of entrances, exits, properties, and dialogue. Gerritsen notes that the main scribe has followed a common practice of folding each sheet vertically twice to provide three columns: the first for speech prefixes, the second for dialogue, and the third for exit directions;[13] however, the folds are no longer easily visible. Speech prefixes thus are ranged left, with the main body of the dialogue presented throughout in an indented column.

In the manuscript, the play is divided into five acts at TLN 4, 704, 1286, 1891, and 2421. Scene divisions are noted only at the beginning of each act. The headings for the act and scene numbers are in Latin; numerals are used for the first and third acts, and the rest are spelled out in words. Act divisions are centred between rules, as are the entrance directions immediately following them. Further entrances and other stage directions are centred between rules at TLN 45, 477, 603–4, 759, 939–42, 1083, 1164, 1451–2, 1523, 1648, 2114–15, 2203–4, 2258, 2530, and 2624–8. All these are written in a larger and bolder italic script than the one used in the rest of the manuscript, with the various elements in them marked off by colons and occasional full stops, as in '*Ent: Amiens: At one doore: Montaigne: and | Veramour. At Another:*' at TLN 603–4 on Fol. 8a. Other entrances and stage directions, similarly punctuated but not always between rules, appear in larger script in

10 Gerritsen, p. xvi.

11 Ibid., pp. xvi–xvii, xix.

12 Ibid., p. xvi.

13 Ibid., p. xx.

the manuscript's left-hand margin, along with the speech prefixes, at TLN 96–7, 255, 330, 369, 532, 585, 821–2, 972–3, 994, 1136, 1149–51, 1193, 1195, 1255–6, 1416–17, 1444, 1561, 1595, 1654–6, 1685–8, 1743–5, 1788–9, 1852, 1854, 1914, 1991, 2082, 2254–6, and 2475. These marginal stage directions tend to be relatively brief.

With the comparatively fuller stage directions at TLN 1149–51, 1416–17, and 1685–8, the scribe has run out of room in the left-hand margin for the speech prefixes and has written them slightly further to the right than their usual place; in the following lines he works his way back slowly to their correct location, giving the page a neater look than if he had immediately returned to the usual place for them. The positioning of these speech prefixes shows that the stage directions were written before the prefixes. The presence of the marginal stage direction at TLN 1595 may explain why TLN 1596–7 are ranged slightly to the left. The entrances at TLN 1193 and 1854 were incorrectly positioned, deleted, and inserted two lines later and two lines earlier, respectively. Two further entrances are marked with directions immediately following speeches at TLN 617 and 2875–6.

Exit directions follow the end of speeches. At TLN 181 and 476, the scribe used the singular '*Exit*' when several characters leave the stage, but at the end of the second Act (TLN 1285) he deleted '*Exit*' and replaced it with '*Exeunt*' and at TLN 2195 deleted '*Exit*' and ended the scene at TLN 2202 with '*Exeunt*'. With the stage direction '*Exit*' he included the name of the character leaving the stage at TLN 170, 179, 367, 575–6, 632–3, 1808–9, 1884, and 2873. When two or more characters leave the stage, the scribe generally wrote '*Exeunt*', as at TLN 602, 703, 1082, 1136, 1163, 1285, 1522, 1647, 2420, 2529, 2623, and 2924. However, on a number of occasions he shortened the form to '*Exe*', once on its own (TLN 758), but more often with the names of the characters added, as at TLN 447–8, 1434, 1731, 2162–3, and 2173. On one occasion, at TLN 1854–5, he wrote '*Ext*' with the characters' names. At TLN 703 and 1522 the scribe has later expanded exit directions from '*Exe*' to '*Exeunt*' or corrected the words in some other way. A few brief stage directions also appear at the end of speeches, at TLN 569 ('*drawes*'), 570 ('*drawes*'), 605 ('*they drawe*'), 1274 ('*they fight*'), 1389 ('*Sighes*'), 1620 ('*drawe both*'), 2052 ('*kneeles*'), and 2363 ('*shootes*'); all are preceded by distinctively drawn braces.

Short single rules are used routinely to separate the speeches of different characters. When changes of speaker coincide with the beginning of a new page the scribe began the page with a short rule.[14] He was less consistent about rules at the end of speeches that occur at the foot of the page, frequently omitting them.[15] When he did supply them, they were then repeated at the head of the following page and hence they appear in this edition as

[14] Fols. 2a, 2b, 4a, 5b, 10b, 12b, 13b, 14a, 14b, 15b, 16a, 17b, 18a, 18b, 20a, 21b, 22b, 24a, 24b, 25a, 26a, 27a, 28b, 31a, 32a, and 33b.

[15] Fols. 1b, 2a, 3b, 12a, 13a, 13b, 14a, 15b, 17b, 19b, 23b, 24a, 25b, 28a, 30b, and 33a.

double rules.[16] On Fol. 31a, at the close of a speech, the page ends with an extended rule which anticipates the stage direction on Fol. 31b.

Longer and wider rules were used, not always consistently, to separate Act divisions from stage directions and to separate stage directions from dialogue. At TLN 2650 and 2700 (Fols. 31b and 32a) the scribe has written the brief dialogue of two or more sets of characters on one line of text. Although the second occurrence has been deleted (it is printed in F1), the first has not been deleted, suggesting that it was a marginal authorial addition that the scribe copied as he saw it. He appears to have written most of his text in the order in which he found it in his copy.

A number of cuts, marked by horizontal lines before and after the deleted dialogue with a vertical line in the margin, appear on Fols. 4a, 16b, 17a, 18a, 20b–21a, 22a, 23b, 24a, 24b, 25a, 31a, and 34b. These cuts occur largely in the speeches of Longaville, Dubois, Montaigne, Charlotte, and particularly Viramour. They appear designed to hasten the main action and to shorten the action or dialogue in the subplots. The deletions made on Fols. 20b–21a required the scribe to move an entrance direction for Montaigne, Lamira, Lady Orleance, Charlot, and the Page from Fol. 21a to Fol. 20b (see Plate 2); he shortened the description by omitting the adjective '*bare*' (TLN 1686), changed the shortened form of Viramour ('*Viram:*'; TLN 1688) to his generic description as 'Page', and neglected to cancel the original entrance. At the end of the cut to Montaigne's speech on Fol. 23b, the scribe has left a blank space which would accommodate a full line of verse. Since no dialogue appears to have been omitted here, Gerritsen concluded that the 'present cut was probably in the copy-text'.[17]

Although all these larger cuts may have been made at any point after the original performance, it is possible, since the last two characters were probably played by boys, that they are the result of less capable boy actors being available for a later revival of the play. However, as these vertical lines marking cuts do not obscure the text, they may have signalled that the passages were not to be cut permanently, but could be omitted whenever required by particular acting conditions. This may help to explain the marginal annotations to the cut, affecting TLN 2911–23, where the scribe has written '*stet:*' three times.

A further cut marked both by horizontal and vertical lines as well as by heavy deletion appears on Fol. 9b (see Plate 3). Other deletions of parts of lines or of stage directions, as opposed to corrections of errors in copying, appear on Fols. 10b (TLN 810–11), 18a (TLN 1451), 19b (TLN 1579–80), 23a (TLN 1881), 28b (TLN 2356), 32a (TLN 2700), 32b (TLN 2733), and 33a (TLN 2793). These remove some of the bawdy language and epithets and the religious oaths in the play. The cut on Fol. 18a removes the reference

[16] Fols. 5a/5b, 10a/10b, 15a/15b, 17a/17b, 18a/18b, 21a/21b, 22a/22b, 24b/25a, 26b/27a, and 31b/32a.

[17] Gerritsen, p. 158.

to a song, although the accompanying stage direction, indicating the song's presence, has not been altered.[18]

The cuts are particularly heavy towards the end of the play: most strikingly, the whole of Act 5 scene 3 in the 1647 Folio, some fifty lines of dialogue, is omitted in the manuscript, its action reduced to a single stage direction '*A Banquet: Set out:*' (TLN 2624). All these cuts point clearly towards the manuscript's theatrical provenance.

The Hands

W. W. Greg's tentative identification of the main scribe of the manuscript as Edward Knight was confirmed by Gerritsen on the basis of Knight's signature at Dulwich College as a witness to the 1616 Articles of Agreement between Edward Alleyn and several players in his employ, notably Jacob Meade.[19] This document appears to record Knight's first connection to the professional theatre. He may have worked as scribe or bookkeeper for Alleyn, who, like his father-in-law Henslowe, used his employees, whenever possible, rather than professional scribes or attorneys, to witness his contracts. At some point after 1616, Knight apparently became the bookkeeper for the King's Men. On 27 December 1624, his name appears in the list made by Sir Henry Herbert, the Master of the Revels, of King's Men's employees.[20]

Knight copied the manuscript of John Fletcher's *Bonduca* (BL Additional MS 36758) and altered Philip Massinger's autograph manuscript of *Believe as You List* (BL Egerton MS 1994) at the behest of Herbert who, in 1631, had objected to its representation of the deposing of King Sebastian of Portugal by the Spanish monarch Philip II. Knight most likely followed Massinger's direction to alter the setting and character names from Spanish to Greek in order to have the play licensed. Around the same time, Knight also annotated the scribal manuscript of *The Soddered Citizen* (Wiltshire Record Office MS 865) probably in collaboration with either the play's author, John Clavell, or with a theatrical reviser.[21] That Knight summarized a missing scene at the beginning of Act 5 of *Bonduca*, rather than trying to write a new one or reconstruct the old one, suggests that he considered his

[18] Cf. *The Control and Censorship of Caroline Drama: The Records of Sir Henry Herbert, Master of the Revels 1623–73*, ed. N. W. Bawcutt (Oxford, 1996), pp. 57–9.

[19] Gerritsen, p. xxii. See Dulwich College Alleyn MSS I, Article 107; *Henslowe Papers Being Documents Supplementary to Henlsowe's Diary*, ed. W. W. Greg (London, 1907), pp. 90–1. Greg's identification was made in W. W. Greg, *Dramatic Documents from the Elizabethan Playhouses*, 2 vols. (Oxford, 1931), i. 233. Documents at Dulwich College referred to in this Introduction are available in digital form through the Henslowe–Alleyn Digitisation Project.

[20] Bentley, i. 15–16.

[21] See *The Soddered Citizen*, ed. J. H. P. Pafford, Malone Society Reprints (Oxford, 1936), p. viii.

role to be that of a conservative editor, not a composing author or a reviser, of play-texts.[22]

Knight wrote the dialogue in *The Honest Man's Fortune* in a clear and professional secretary hand containing some italic letters, but he did not use such letters consistently.[23] For example, his alternation of italic and secretary forms of *r* and *t* is arbitrary, although he was fairly consistent in using secretary long *s* in initial and medial positions and a spurred *a* when it appears in the initial position. Some of his minuscule letters, particularly *y* and *g*, are so elaborately formed as to suggest that he was writing slowly and deliberately: he has taken some pains to write out these letters, even when they occur in a medial position and are thus not easily linked to the next letter. He used a number of forms of secretary *h* with the ascender and descender varying notably in size. Sometimes he produced a small flourish on the final letter in a word, regardless of whether it has an ascender or descender, except in the case of a final *e* following a *t* in which the *e* is only partly formed, as with 'sute' at TLN 1677 and 'parte' at 1683 on Fol. 20b (see Plate 3). Knight used italic for speech prefixes and stage directions and for proper names within the dialogue. He increased the number of lines to the page towards the end of the manuscript, but used dark-brown ink throughout.[24]

Knight was consistent in using the following abbreviations with superscript letters: o^{r} (our), o^{rs}(ours), y^{or} (your), yo^{rs} and yo^{res} (yours), w^{th} (with), $w^{th}out$ (without), and w^{ch} (which). Although Gerritsen did not render the letters *h*, *s*, and *t* in these brevigraphs as superscript, they are indeed written above the line of text, although slightly lower than the superscript letters which precede them. Knight used a long macron over abbreviations of a medial *m*, as in 'becom̃ing' or 'som̃e' (TLN 212, 423). Usually the macron extends before and after the letter being abbreviated, although Knight was inconsistent in where he placed two small vertical lines crossing it through; sometimes this mark appears over the *o*, sometimes over the *m*. His abbreviations for 'gentlemen' or 'gentlewomen' are almost always rendered as '$\overline{\text{gent}}$' with a macron over all the letters (for example, at TLN 786, 899).

At least three other seventeenth-century hands appear in the manuscript.[25] An unidentified, predominantly italic hand, here named Hand 2, is presumably that of a theatrical reviser. Hand 2 has made some minor alterations to the manuscript (see TLN 1815, 2813, and perhaps 2791) and two more significant additions. On Fol. 20b he has interlined a line of dialogue (TLN

[22] For a transcription of this scene, see *Bonduca by John Fletcher*, ed. W. W. Greg, Malone Society Reprints (Oxford, 1951), p. 90.

[23] For a parallel discussion of Knight's characteristics as scribe and bookkeeper, see *Bonduca*, pp. vi–ix.

[24] See Gerritsen, p. xx.

[25] This analysis is essentially the same as Gerritsen's (pp. xxviii–xxxi). He designated Hands A1, A2, and A3, as Knight's English, italic, and bold italic scripts, respectively; Hand B is that of the theatrical reviser; Hand C wrote the name 'Ihon' at TLN 2926; Hand D is the hand of Sir Henry Herbert.

1656) to provide a new cue line to cover a large cut. On Fol. 25b, he has turned the page 180 degrees counter-clockwise to insert a line (TLN 2093) in the left-hand margin, marking both the addition and the place of insertion with an 'X' (see Plate 4). This hand may also have been responsible for the cuts in the manuscript. The licence that Herbert (Hand 4) wrote on Fol. 34b (see Plate 5) is preceded by another hand (Hand 3) that wrote the name 'Ihon', drawing a nearly complete oval circle from the top of the ascender of the first letter. A further, modern hand, probably that of Dyce, added a few words in pencil, including '__ here' in the right-hand margin of a line of dialogue at TLN 1796 (Fol. 22a). This modern hand probably also added in pen the foliation where the original has been lost, as well as 'x Taylor' followed by a long slash, to replace the licence's missing name of the actor Joseph Taylor, a prominent member and business manager of the King's Men.[26]

Knight's spelling is consistent with the orthography of the period and among his preferred forms are: 'hir' (for 'her'; TLN 27, 587, etc.), 'agen' (for 'again'; TLN 124, 565, etc.), 'wolld' (for 'would', TLN 12, 40, etc.), 'frend' (TLN 40, 480, etc.) and 'frend*es*' (TLN 382, 383, etc.), 'falce' (TLN 1411, 2078, etc.) and 'falcer' (TLN 2303), 'hansome' (TLN 2461, 2464, etc.), 'perceaue' (TLN 490, 548, etc.), 'sodaine' (TLN 1087, 1214), 'woeman' (TLN 633, 1885, etc.) and 'woemans' (TLN 1791, 2175). In some cases he routinely transposes letters, as in 'lenght' (TLN 1640, 1659) and 'strenght' (TLN 297, 464, etc.). He frequently uses a 'w' in place of 'u' when in medial or final position in a word, as in 'prowde' (TLN 553, 1468, etc.), 'continew' (TLN 682, 1765), 'perswasion(s)' (TLN 251, 2891), 'rowze' (TLN 2021), 'sawce' (TLN 2558), and 'sawsiges' (TLN 1283). He makes frequent use of the symbol for 'es' at the end of the word, particularly in 'that*es*' (TLN 50, 84, etc.) and 'what*es*' (TLN 377, 831, etc.). He is given to doubling consonants in words such as 'spiritt*es*' (TLN 756, 1193, etc.; but cf. 'spirit*es*' at TLN 2153) and 'gutt*es*' (TLN 766, 1282; but cf. 'gut*es*' at TLN 2387). He omits the *e* in the past tense of a word, as in 'followd' (TLN 229, 752), unless it is stressed metrically. Some of his more unusual spellings are 'garsoon' (for 'garçon'; TLN 1597), 'Incorrage' (for 'encourage'; TLN 409), and 'meich' (for 'meech'; TLN 2541).

In stage directions and dialogue he uses alternative spellings of characters' names, as with '*Montaigne*' (TLN 45, 63, etc.) and '*Montagne*' (TLN 821, 823, etc.), '*Lapoop*' (TLN 759, 760, etc.) and '*Lapoope*' (TLN 1150, 1271, etc.), '*Lamira*' (TLN 691, 866, etc.) and '*Lamyra*' (TLN 1434, 1686, etc.), and '*Charlot*' (TLN 1416, 1656, etc.) and '*Charlote*' (TLN 1419, 1434, etc.), but never '*Charlotte*'. '*Monsieur*' is commonly rendered as '*Monsir*' in stage directions and in dialogue (TLN 878, 932, etc.). In speech prefixes, he is inconsistent in writing out the full name of the character or abbreviating it; his abbreviations of the same name are also inconsistent. Knight is particularly heavy in his use of parentheses and punctuation marks, including

[26] On Taylor's career see Bentley, ii. 590–8.

question and exclamation marks, but he is inconsistent in distinguishing between commas and full stops, even at the end of characters' speeches. When writing a number, he almost always uses a small raised point before and after it, as in '·*2*·' (TLN 100, 105, etc.) or just after it as in '12·' (TLN 871).

He added abbreviated forms of the names of three actors in stage directions: George Vernon's and John Rhodes's names appear at TLN 370 (Fol. 5a) in the entrance directions for '*ye Creditors*', and George Rickner's name appears at TLN 477 (Fol. 6b) in an entrance for Orleance's servant. Vernon, Rhodes, and Rickner were named along with Knight in the 27 December 1624 list of men 'imployed by the Kinges Maties servantes in theire quallity of Playinge as Musitions and other necessary attendantes'. However, Bentley argued that none of the three actors was a full member of the company in 1624–5, but that they were probably all hired men used to fill in roles as necessary.[27]

The Play

The manuscript's title-page carries the notation '*Plaide In the yeare 1613:*'. In his licence at the end of the manuscript (Fol. 34b), Herbert noted: '*This Play. being an olde One and the Originall Lost was reallowd by mee. This: 8. febru.* <u>*1624*</u>', that is, 1625. Herbert's official records provide a similar account: 'For the Kgs comp: an olde P. call: The honests mans fortune the original being lost was reallowed by mee att Mr. Taylors intreaty & on condition to give me a booke 8th. Feb: 1624'.[28] The book provided as payment for this relicensing was evidently a printed copy of Sir Philip Sidney's prose romance *The Countess of Pembroke's Arcadia*. Greg and Gerritsen each argued from the form of Herbert's notes here that this manuscript of *The Honest Man's Fortune* was newly copied just prior to 8 February 1625 and that the lost original was the copy, carrying the original licence, which had been allowed in 1613, when the play was 'Plaide' as the title-page notes.[29]

However, there is some evidence to suggest that this copy could have been made earlier than 1625. The note on the title-page in Knight's mixed-secretary and italic hand of '*Plaide In the yeare 1613:*' is in a different ink

[27] Bentley, i, 15–16, ii, 544–6, 547, 611–12.

[28] Bawcutt, p. 160.

[29] See Greg, *Dramatic Documents from the Elizabethan Playhouses*, pp. 289–90, where he argued that the Dyce manuscript was copied from a theatrical manuscript, not from foul papers; he argued a year earlier in 'A Question of Plus or Minus', *Review of English Studies*, 6 (1930), 300–4, at p. 303, that the Dyce manuscript 'was prepared for relicence by Herbert, 8 February, 1624/5'. Gerritsen noted of the Dyce manuscript, 'From the licence it appears to have been written at the beginning of 1625' (p. xvii). He added that within a month of the 27 December 1624 document listing Knight as a member of the King's Company, Knight 'was completing his transcript of *The Honest mans Fortune*' (p. xxiii). Gerritsen accepted Taylor's 'veracity' in assuming that the 'original licensed prompt-book' was lost and that the Dyce manuscript was a new copy in 1625 of extant foul papers (pp. xlv–lxviii). Hoy, Textual Introduction, pp. 5–8, also assumed that the Dyce manuscript was newly copied in 1625. But he argued unconvincingly that although the Folio text is 'maddeningly unprofessional' and a 'wretched job of printing', it is superior to the Dyce manuscript in preserving accidentals of the authorial foul papers that presumably served as copy for both texts.

from that of the italic title '*The Honest mans Fortune*' (see Plate 1). This may signify that the title-page and the entire manuscript had been in existence prior to its relicensing and only the notation '*Plaide In the yeare 1613:*' on the title-page was added immediately prior to 1625. At some point the manuscript was damaged, resulting in the loss of Taylor's name in the licence and of the leaf numbers for Fols. 1, 2, 3, 33, and 34: both elements have been restored in a modern hand which may be Dyce's.[30] If the manuscript was copied immediately prior to 8 February 1625, it could have suffered the damage sometime before Dyce's purchase of it from the Heber sale. However, Knight began working with the King's Men in 1616, after having been employed by Henslowe, who had commissioned the play for the Lady Elizabeth's Men by 1613. This may suggest that Knight copied out this manuscript at any time during his service with Henslowe or shortly afterwards, and that the manuscript already had some slight damage by 1625. Knight could have added the title-page notation about the play being '*Plaide In the yeare 1613:*' in 1625 to emphasize to Herbert that the play was indeed 'olde' and had been previously licensed.

Although Herbert demanded that legible copies be submitted to him in the case of a revival, he did not require that the copies be new.[31] Scholarly arguments that insist that a new copy had to be made before submission to the censor in 1625 rest on an outdated notion that companies could not afford to keep more than one complete fair copy of a manuscript and that that one copy could only be the licensed copy. Given the survival of so many fair copies of dramatic manuscripts that show signs of theatrical use but which lack the censor's licence, it is reasonable to argue that companies kept at least two complete copies of the company 'book'—the licensed copy and a transcript of it. In fact, for some period of time, whether some years before or immediately prior to 1625, the King's Men had at least two manuscripts of *The Honest Man's Fortune* available to them: Dyce and the source manuscript. This source manuscript was also used at some point, long before or immediately prior to 1647, to make the Folio printer's copy. Thus, if the manuscript used as printer's copy for F1 was made immediately prior to its printing, the source copy must have survived for many years until 1647. If

[30] As Gerritsen, p. xxxi, noted, the marginal addition of Taylor's name 'was probably supplied from Herbert's record of the licence, printed by Malone'.

[31] As Bawcutt noted, Herbert 'seems to have been fairly tolerant' in reading any 'untidy and hard to read' manuscripts submitted to him (p. 42). He complained only occasionally about illegible or extraordinarily long manuscripts. On 21 October 1633, Herbert demanded of acting companies that 'The Master ought to have copies of their new playes left with him, that he may be able to shew what he hath allowed or disallowed' and that 'All ould plays ought to bee brought to the Master of the Revells, and have his allowance to them for which he should have his fee' (p. 182). Although Herbert could have demanded here that these 'ould plays' be newly copied for relicensing, he did not do so, nor did he do so in any record before or after 1633. Given his own experience as censor and as a theatre-company manager, Herbert would have been aware that older copies of plays would have been more comprehensive than newly made copies in showing the plays' performance history in terms of cuts, additions, and other alterations that had the potential to cause problems.

the F1 copy was not made earlier than in 1646, it may have been extant for many years. It is possible that the King's Men had access at a given time to all three manuscripts: the source copy, Dyce, and the F1 copy.

Greg contended in 1931 that the Dyce manuscript 'does not give the impression of having been prepared from "foul papers" like that of *Bonduca*'. However, in 1952, Gerritsen argued that this manuscript and that serving as printer's copy for the 1647 Folio text were both copied from foul papers.[32] Greg's dismissal of foul-paper copy for this manuscript may be supported by the likelihood that Henslowe, who commissioned plays for the Lady Elizabeth's Men, the company for whom the play was written in 1612–13, did not accept foul-paper copies of completed plays from dramatists. As a series of letters from Robert Daborne to Henslowe in 1613–14 makes clear, Daborne was to submit in every instance of a contracted play the 'fayr' and not the 'Foule' sheet in order to be paid.[33] Hence, the foul papers of a dispersed group of collaborators most likely would not have been available some years after the play's composition, nor would they have been readily available in another company's inventory for recopying in 1625 as Gerritsen posited.

How the play moved from the Lady Elizabeth's Men to the King's Men's repertory is not clear. The 1679 second folio of Beaumont and Fletcher's works provides a list of the original actors in the play as Nathan Field, Joseph Taylor, Robert Benfield, William Eccleston, Emanuel Reade, and Thomas Basse.[34] Field most likely left the Lady's Elizabeth's Men in 1616 to join the King's Men and died in 1620. Taylor moved from the Lady Elizabeth's Men, which he had joined in 1611, to Prince Charles's Men in 1616 and then to the King's Men in 1619. Eccleston moved from the King's to the Lady Elizabeth's Men in 1611, returning to the King's Men in 1613, and seems to have retired by 1623. Benfield moved from the Lady Elizabeth's Men to the King's Men by 1616.[35] Thus, any or all of these men could have taken the play to the King's Men much earlier than 1625 but they would have needed permission to do so.

Upon Henslowe's death in 1616, Alleyn inherited not only his businesses but his theatrical properties and goods, including playbooks such as this one. Alleyn stayed on friendly terms with many of his former colleagues, and, in fact, records dining with Taylor in 1618 and 1619.[36] Henslowe kept such a tight financial control on the Lady Elizabeth's Men that in 1615 they drew up articles of grievance against him accusing him of forcing them into

[32] Greg, *Dramatic Documents from the Elizabethan Playhouses*, p. 290; Gerritsen, pp. xlv–lxviii.

[33] See Grace Ioppolo, '"The Foule Sheet and ye fayr": Henslowe, Daborne, Heywood and the Nature of Foul-Paper and Fair-Copy Dramatic Manuscripts', *English Manuscript Studies*, 11 (2002), 132–53.

[34] Francis Beaumont and John Fletcher, *Fifty Comedies and Tragedies* (London, 1679), sig. ^{2}3S3^{r}.

[35] Bentley, ii. 435, 591, 429, 374.

[36] See 'The Diary of Edward Alleyn', in William Young, *The History of Dulwich College*, 2 vols. (Edinburgh, 1889), ii. 109, 147.

debt.[37] So it is doubtful that the actors tried to claim the financial right to the play without paying him for it. Nor would they have considered their financial obligations to Henslowe to have ended with his death. Instead, they would have sought Alleyn's formal or informal permission to transfer the financial rights to the play to another company, even as late as 1625, since Alleyn was still alive.

As Taylor was the one who entreated Herbert in 1625 to believe that the original licensed copy, presumably signed by George Buc, was lost, it may have been Taylor who took the play manuscript to his later company. Knight, who was employed by the King's Men after 1616, may have also played some role in persuading the King's Men to revive it or Herbert to relicense it. In fact, Herbert's licence lacks his signature, and as Bawcutt noted, it is 'unlikely that he minutely inspected the play, since it contains numerous oaths that he would have deleted'.[38] However, as Hoy points out, the Dyce manuscript uses the word 'Heaven' in numerous places in which F1 uses the word 'God',[39] suggesting that Knight purged some oaths in copying it, either at his own discretion or in following his copy.

Thus, at some point between 1616 and 1625, Alleyn or Henslowe almost certainly sold the play to the King's Men, or otherwise allowed them permission to perform it, and gave them access to a full text of it. Since the play was new to the company, they had to follow Herbert's instructions and have it licensed for a revival in 1625. Herbert's records as Lord Chamberlain show that he maintained cordial relations both with the King's Men's actors and with Knight himself, so Herbert may simply have trusted Taylor and Knight, whose hand he may have recognized, that there was nothing troublesome in the play, and licensed the manuscript without reading it carefully.

Authorship

Although the play was attributed to Beaumont and Fletcher in F1, scholars have generally agreed that Fletcher was a part-author of the play, but they have been divided on the number and the identities of his collaborators. F. G. Fleay, whose nineteenth-century scholarship was largely discredited in the early twentieth century, attributed the play to Fletcher, Massinger, Field, and Daborne.[40] Gerritsen challenged attribution studies of the play by E. H. C. Oliphant[41] and used stylistic tests to argue that Cyril Tourneur wrote most of Acts 1 and 2, with Nathan Field writing Acts 3 and 4, and

[37] Dulwich College Alleyn MSS 1, Article 106; *Henslowe Papers*, pp. 86–90.

[38] Bawcutt, p. 58. [39] Hoy, Textual Introduction, p. 5.

[40] Frederick Gard Fleay, *A Biographical Chronicle of the English Drama 1559–1642*, 2 vols. (London, 1891), i. 77, 81.

[41] Oliphant, in *The Plays of Beaumont and Fletcher: An Attempt to Determine their Respective Shares and the Shares of Others* (New Haven, Conn., 1927), p. 385, broke down the shares of the play this way: Tourneur: Act 1, 2.1, and 2.3; Webster: 2.2, 2.4a, 3.1b, 3.2b, 3.2d, 3.3b, 3.3d, 3.3f; Field: 2.4b, Act 4, 5.3b; Fletcher: 5.1–3a; Massinger: 3.2a, 3.2c, 3.3a, 3.3c, 3.3e; Webster and Massinger: 3.1a, 3.1c.

Fletcher contributing Act 5. In the process, Gerritsen dismissed Massinger, Webster, and Daborne as collaborators or part-authors in the play.[42] However, in 1959, on stylistic grounds Cyrus Hoy attributed Acts 1, 2, 4, the second half of 3.1, and all of 3.2 to Field, 5.1 and 5.4 to Field and Fletcher, 3.3 to Field and Massinger, 5.2 and 5.3 to Fletcher, and the first part of 3.1 to Massinger.[43] These and other attribution studies have also considered one piece of external evidence for attribution, namely an undated letter of about 1613, from Field, Massinger, and Daborne to Henslowe, asking for a £5 advance on the £10 owed them, as Daborne says, 'for the play of m^r^ ffletcher & owrs'.[44]

Scholars have rejected the idea that Daborne wrote any part of the play largely on the grounds that he was a hack writer who eventually abandoned playwriting for a career in the church.[45] However, Daborne was already under contract to write four other plays for Henslowe in 1613 and 1614, and in fact, assigned one act of his play *The Arraignment of London* to Tourneur in order to complete it on time.[46] So it would not be surprising that Daborne, a chief dramatist for the Lady Elizabeth's Men and privy to their plans and schedules, as his letters attest, proposed himself at least as a collaborator with Fletcher. As Field and Massinger were still new to playwriting in 1613, Fletcher and Daborne may have been the senior writers at the commissioning of *The Honest Man's Fortune*, with the less-experienced pair of men intended to serve as their junior collaborators. Fletcher and Field collaborated on *Four Plays in One* and, together with Massinger, on *The Knight of Malta*, *The Queen of Corinth*, and the lost *The Jeweller of Amsterdam*.[47]

As Henslowe's Diary and his later correspondence with dramatists amply demonstrate, collaborators might shift not once but sometimes many times during the composition of any given play. Henslowe paid a small advance to authors when commissioning them, another advance with the submission of some part of their text, or even the promise of it, and the last payment only when final copy was received. In numerous cases, some original collaborators dropped out after receiving enough of an advance to offset immediate financial problems and were replaced by other authors, so that those who finally submitted their completed portions of a play, most usually one or more acts, may not have been those initially commissioned. Thus the letter to Henslowe cited above suggests that Fletcher had as his original collaborators Field, Daborne, and Massinger, and that one or more may have been

[42] Gerritsen, pp. lxviii–xciv.

[43] Cyrus Hoy, 'The Shares of Fletcher and his Collaborators in the Beaumont and Fletcher Canon (IV)', *Studies in Bibliography*, 12 (1959), 91–116, especially pp. 100–8. See also the Textual Introduction to his edition of the play, where he notes, for example, that most cuts in the manuscript text originated in 1625 (p. 6).

[44] Dulwich College Alleyn MSS I, Article 68; *Henslowe Papers*, pp. 65–7; cf. Gerritsen, p. lxix.

[45] See, for example, Gerritsen, p. lxix.

[46] Dulwich College Alleyn MSS I, Article 78; *Henslowe Papers*, pp. 71–2.

[47] Hoy, Textual Introduction, pp. 3–4.

replaced.[48] If Fletcher was the senior writer at the play's completion, he may have helped join the acts fairly seamlessly or otherwise overseen the collaboration. In any case, even though the play's authorship may never be definitely established, its major themes, characters, structure, and style are sufficiently consistent to produce a coherent text.

Peformance, Revision, and Context

As Hoy noted, the Dyce manuscript shows us 'the text of *The Honest Man's Fortune* in the process of being prepared for the stage'.[49] However, this process may have begun before 1625. The play was originally acted in 1613 by the Lady Elizabeth's Men, who at that time usually performed at the Swan Theatre and from 1614 at the Hope Theatre, owned by Henslowe and Alleyn. The play was apparently revived in 1625 by the King's Men, who played both at the second Globe Theatre and at Blackfriars. The only other extant evidence for the play's performance history derives from Herbert's records as the Master of the Revels.

The varying types of cuts, only some of which obscure the manuscript, suggest that the text underwent revision more than once, and that these cuts produced slight adjustments in lines before or after them. Some revisions, including some within cuts to Viramour's speeches, clearly appear to result from problems in performance, as at TLN 1378–87 on Fol. 17a and 1919–41 on Fol. 23b. The original scribe seems to have been working in response to changes made by one or more authors, rather than attempting to revise the play himself. This internal evidence and the external evidence cited above imply that the play could have been revised while still in the repertory of the first company in 1613 and that it was then updated for its revival by the King's Men twelve years later. More importantly, the revisions may demonstrate that the company did not consider this, or any other play-text, to be in a fixed or final state but fluid enough to exist in different versions at different times and in different playing conditions. This may be why the Folio text includes an extra scene between TLN 2623 and 2624 in which four unnamed servants joke about Lamira while setting out a banquet for her guests, as well as twenty-four extra lines on Lauerdure's foolishness that appear between TLN 2919 and 2920. All these self-contained passages are easily detachable from the text.

If the Dyce manuscript was copied before the King's Men acquired it, its revisions and alterations may reflect some aspects of performance before 1625 and not after it, although minor alterations, including the few lines inserted by Hand 2, could have been added immediately before its relicensing in February 1625. The rather awkward later insertions of the names of

[48] In his Textual Introduction, p. 3, Hoy appears to suggest that Field came up with the idea of writing the play, and he 'turned for aid' to Fletcher; but the letter to Henslowe suggests that Fletcher was the original author.

[49] Hoy, Textual Introduction, p. 8.

George Vernon, John Rhodes, and George Rickner alongside or above existing stage directions suggest that the manuscript had already been copied before they joined the company and that they were substituting for actors used in earlier productions before or after February 1625. Knight's insertions point towards his work as a prompter at later performances of the play in which he had to ready the three hired-in, and probably inexperienced, actors for their entrances, rather than company members whose habits he knew well and with whom he had worked before.

Although Greg and Gerritsen argued that the revisions marked by horizontal and vertical lines in the margin represent artistic cuts by the company and that scored-through deletions represent the censor's demands for revision, no such clear distinction can be made. Only some portions of heavily deleted text appear to have been censored, and there are more politically dangerous passages than these throughout the play which have not been altered. More significantly, in his licence Herbert did not demand any cuts, revisions, or alterations, as he did on occasion with other play-texts that he read. What can be safely assumed is that the play underwent revision at various times and that the adjustments made to the text, as on Fols. 21b and 22a, suggest the hand of an observant bookkeeper such as Knight.

It remains impossible precisely to date the Dyce manuscript using internal and external evidence or to trace the play's performance history from 1625. That the play was blocked from being printed in 1641 does not signal that it had been particularly successful in performance, only that the King's Men were determined to protect their repertory. But it is not necessary to assume that the Dyce manuscript was copied immediately prior to its relicensing in 1625, especially given Knight's connections to the actors and financiers of the Lady Elizabeth's Men for whom the play was commissioned twelve years earlier. What is safe to assume is that the Dyce manuscript was copied at some time, and perhaps many years, before 8 February 1625. At least one of two other manuscripts of the play also survived intact for a long period: that used as printer's copy for F1 or that used as source copy for Dyce and the F1 copy. For many years the King's Men kept relatively similar manuscripts of the same play, each showing varying forms of theatrical revision, suggesting that for authors, actors, censors, and audience there was no single and final form of a play-text.

Editorial Conventions

The following conventions are used in this edition. Square brackets enclose deletions, except for those around folio numbers ([Fol. 1a], etc.). Angle brackets enclose material which other causes (paper damage or loss) have removed or made difficult or impossible to decipher. Dots indicate illegible characters (thus '[fall.e]' at TLN 778).

Line numbering for the play is continuous, from Fol. 0a to 34b and indicated by Through Line Numbers (TLNs). Interlineations have been lowered into the text, and noted in the textual apparatus. The position of elements of the text such as speech-prefixes, stage directions, headings, and indentations is reproduced as exactly as type permits. Slight misalignments have been ignored. Rules and dashes have been printed in the text. The text is printed continuously, eliminating the blank line between TLN 1908 and 1909.

As with any transcription, several letter shapes require editorial decisions, especially in distinguishing between majuscule and minuscule forms. For example, it is often difficult to distinguish between majuscule and minuscule 'o' in primary position; this letter has been rendered as a majuscule in Orleans's and Lady Orleans's names when they appear in speech prefixes, stage directions, and dialogue. Superscript letters have been printed in the same size as the remainder of the text. As Knight has been inconsistent in fully forming commas and full stops or periods, the following convention has been used: when the punctuation mark has a tail, it has been rendered as a comma: when it lacks a tail and is either a rounded dot or a slightly vertical line, it has been rendered as a full stop. The position of punctuation above or below the line has been normalized: raised points before and after numerals have been retained in their medial position. Irregularities of word-division are generally ignored. Long *s* has been lowered. With the exception of the final –*e*s, abbreviated forms of words have not been expanded and contractions are printed as they appear in the manuscript.

The pages in the Plates have been reproduced at 82 per cent of full size.

*

The editor wishes to express her thanks to the following: the staff of the National Art Library of the Victoria and Albert Museum for assisting with her study of the original manuscript; the Malone Society for their award of a bursary to fund the illustrations and the permissions to reproduce them; and most especially to H. R. Woudhuysen and G. R. Proudfoot for their generous advice and support.

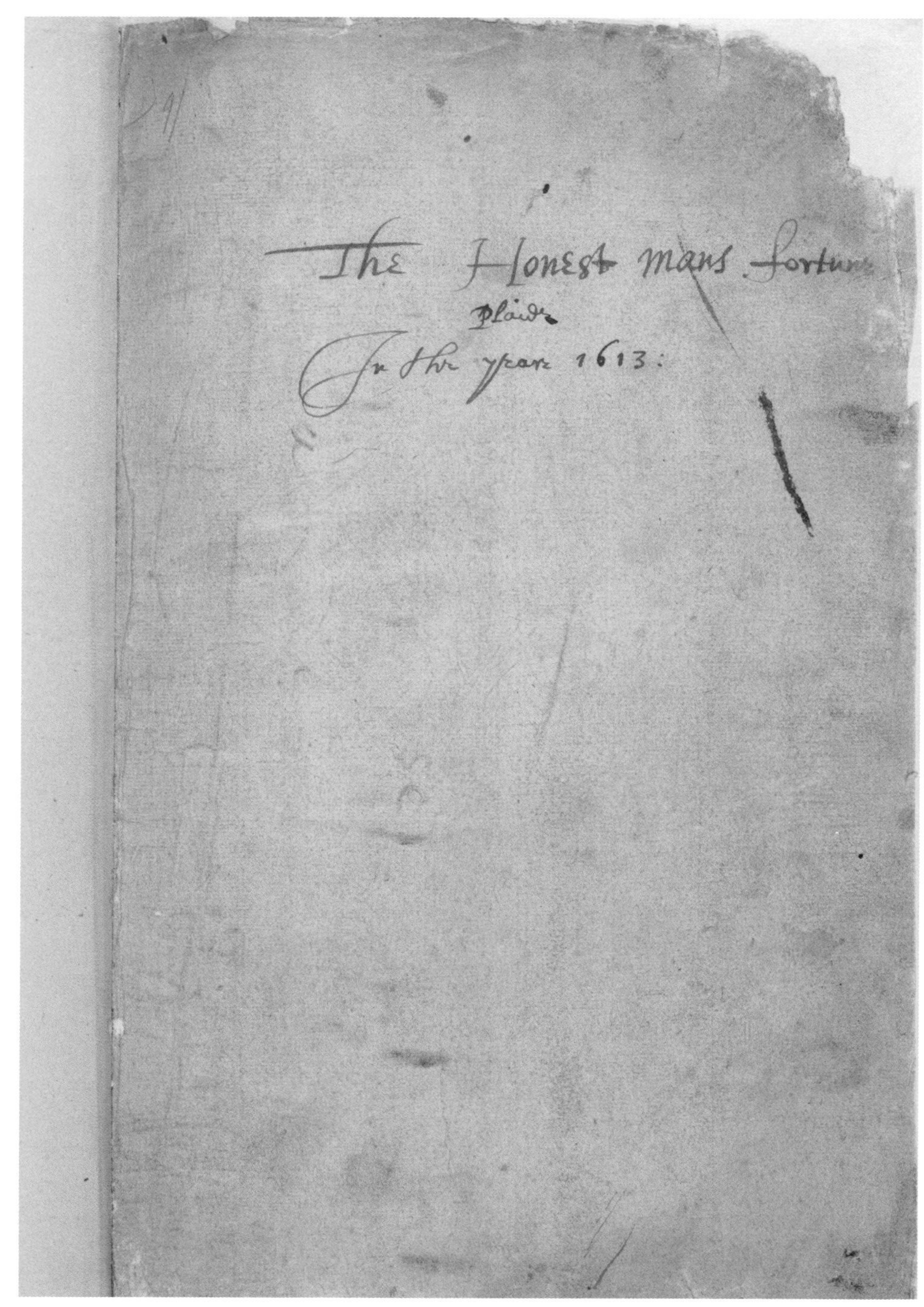

The Honest mans fortune
Plaide
In the yeare 1613:

PLATE 1: FOL. 0a, LINES 1–3

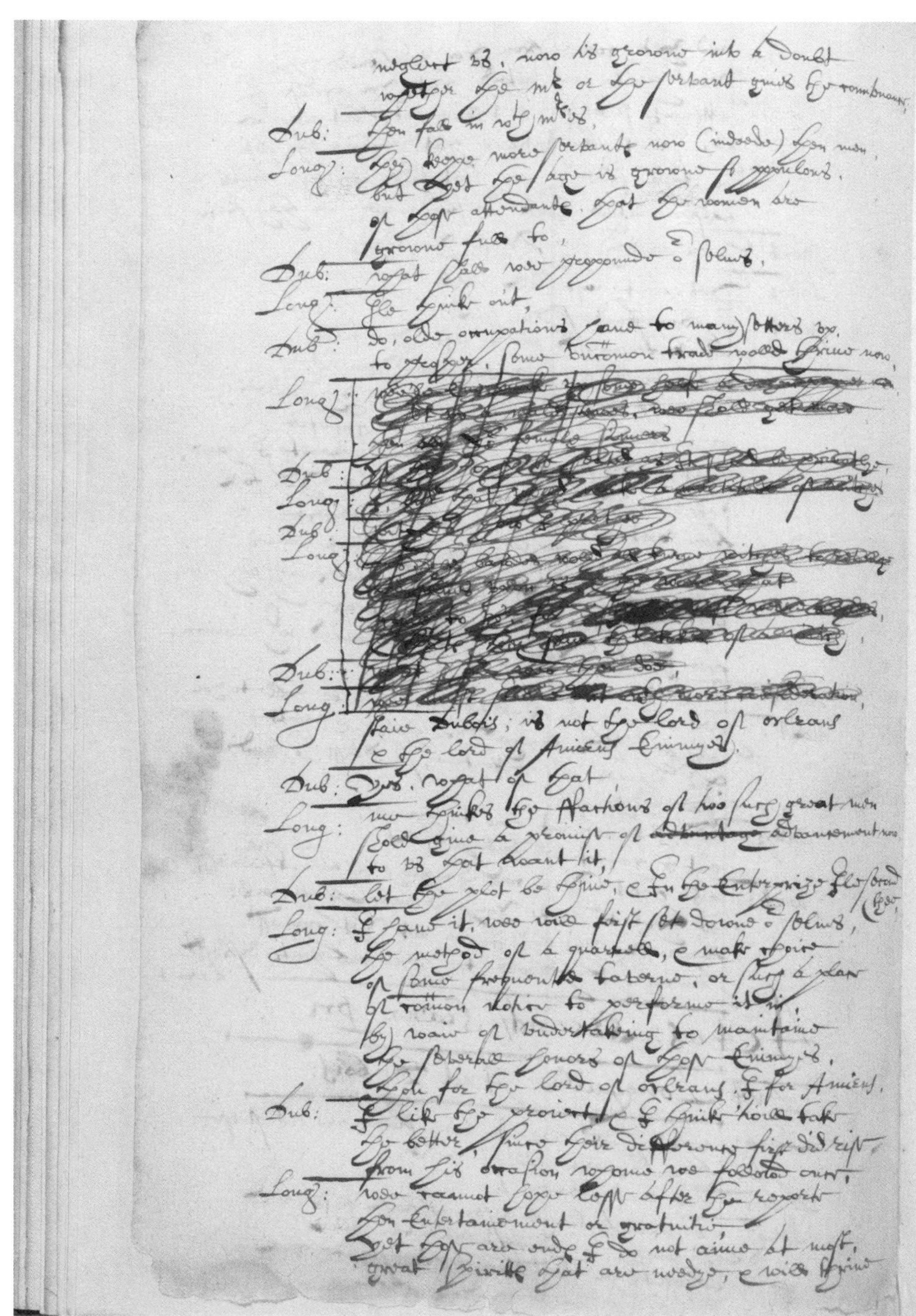

PLATE 2: FOL. 9b, LINES 712–56

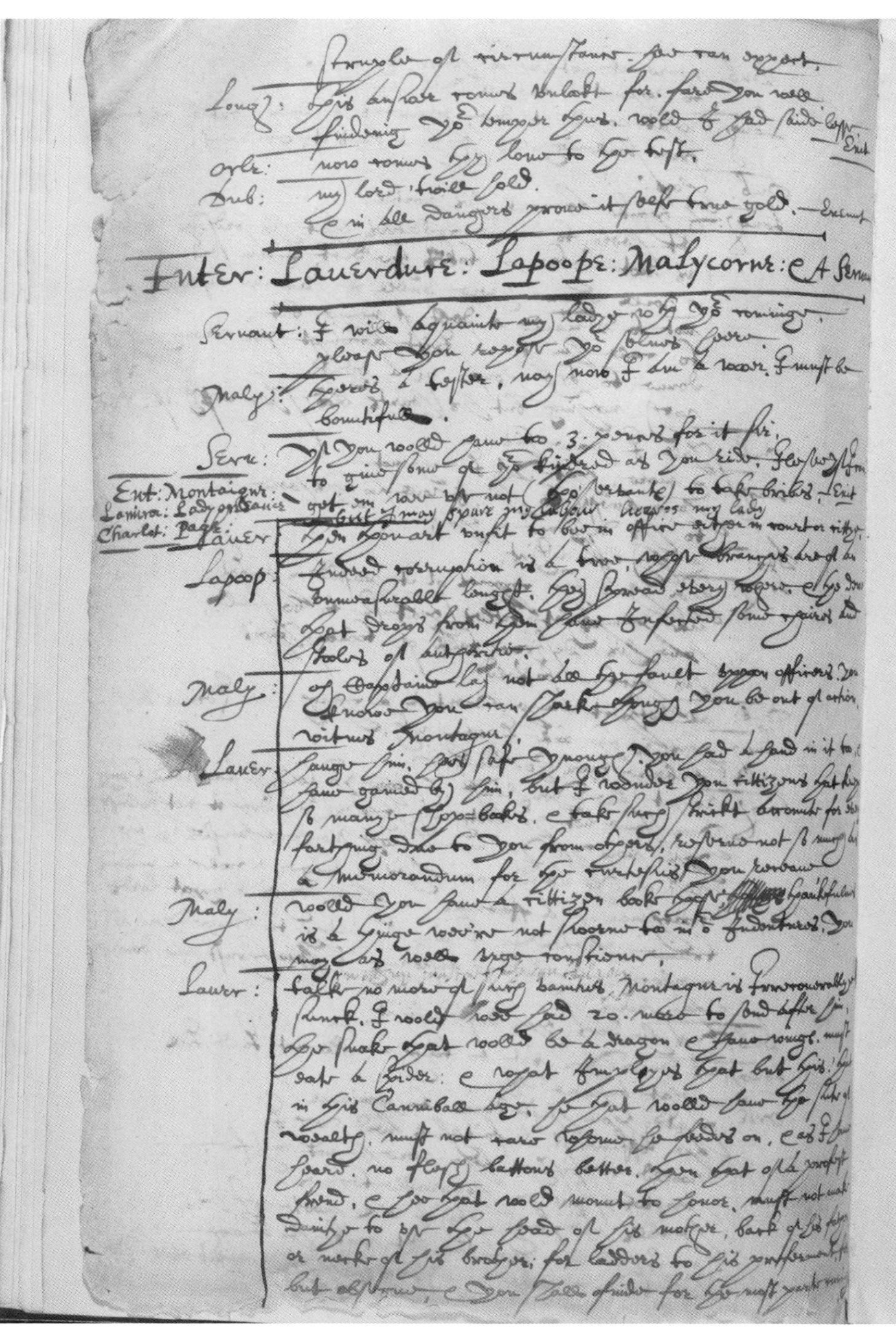

PLATE 3: FOL. 20b, LINES 1641–83

PLATE 4: FOL. 25b, LINES 2081–124

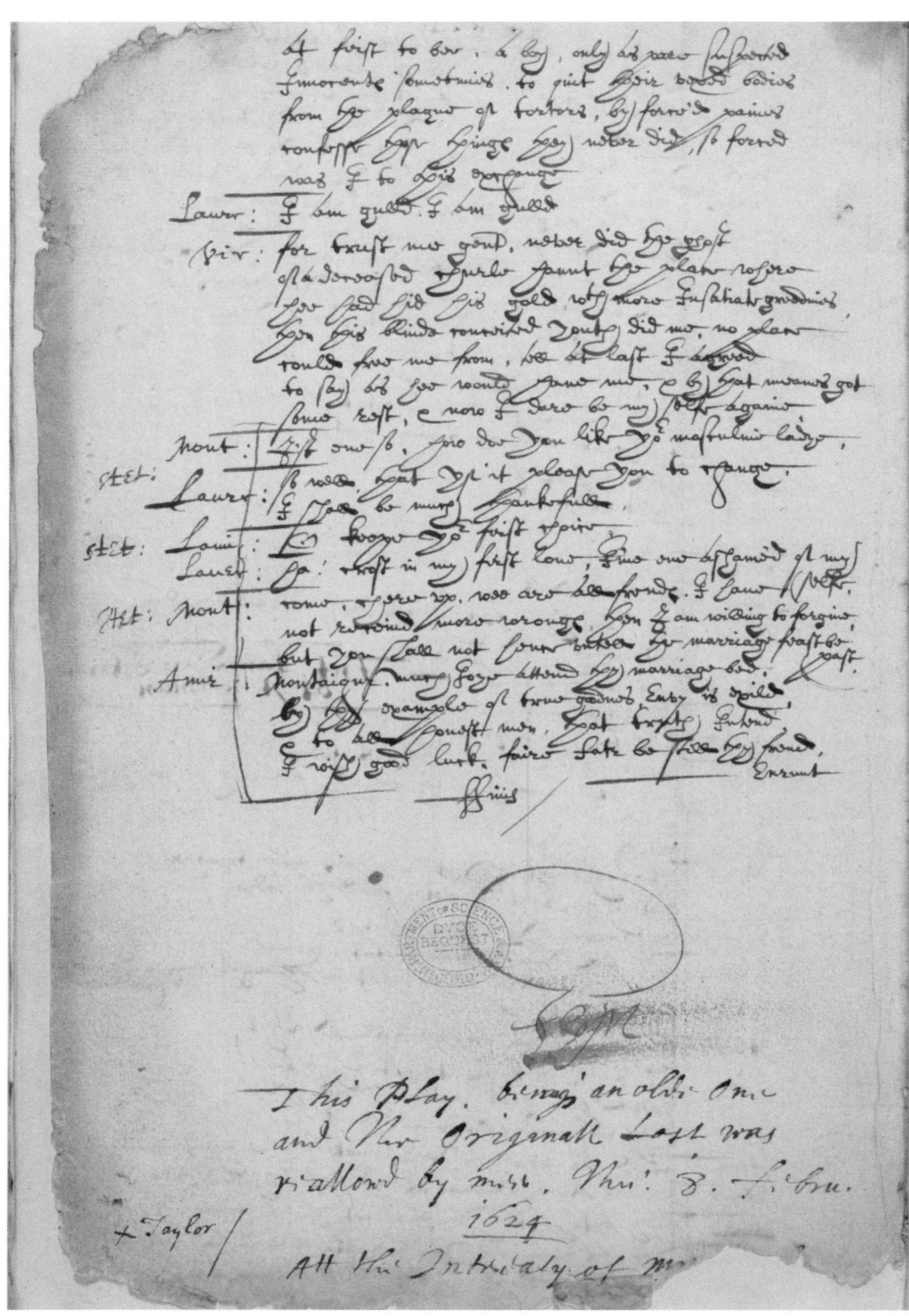
Exeunt

ffinis

This Play, being an olde One
and the Originall Lost was
reallowed by mee. this 8. febru.
1624

Att the Intreaty of Mr Taylor /

PLATE 5: FOL. 34b, LINES 2898–931

[Fol. 0a]

The Honest mans Fortune

Plaide

In the yeare 1613:

[Fol. 0b blank]

Actus: 1: Scæna: 1: [Fol. 1a]

Enter Orleans: And Amiens At Seuerall doores:

Amie: morrow my lord of *Orleans*:

Orle: you salute me
like a strainger, brother *Orleans*
were to me a title more belonging.
whome you call the husband of yor sister.

Amie: wolld the circumstances of or brotherhood
had never offerd cause to make or conversation
lesse familiar; but I mete you like a hinderance
in yor waie, yor great lawe suite is now vpon the
tongue, & ready for a Iudgment,

Orle: came you from the hall now,

Amie: wthout stay. the court is full.
& such a presse of people does attend
the Issue, as yf some great man were brought
to his arraignment,

Orle: Every mothers sonne
of all that multitude of hearers, went
to be a witnes of the missery
yor sisters ffortunes must haue come to
yf my adversary who did loue her first
had beene hir husband.

Amie: the successe may drawe a testmonye from them
to confirme the same oppinion, but they went
prepard wth no such hope or purpose,

Orle: & did you Entreate the number of them
that are gone wth no such purpose,

Amie: tush. yor owne experience of my heart
can answer you,

Orle: This doubtfull [question] answer
makes me clearly vnderstand yor disposition.

4] folio number (⟨*1*⟩ above and to the right of this; folio number *1* added in a modern hand 31 *them*] *m* altered

University of Nevada, Reno

Dear Malone Society Member,

Enclosed is the current Malone Society Publication, volume 176 (published in 2012 for 2009), an edition of *The Honest Man's Fortune*, which you are receiving because you were a member in 2009.

Eric Rasmussen

Department of English/0098
College of Liberal Arts
University of Nevada, Reno
Reno, Nevada 89557-0098
(775) 784-6689 office
(775) 784-6266 fax

Amie: yf yor cause be Iust,
I wish you a conclusion like yor cause.

Orle: I can haue any cōmon charitye to such a prayer,
from a frend I wolld expect a love to what
I prosper in: wthout exceptions, such a[s] loue
as might make all my vndertakeing*es* thankfull too't
precisely Iust, is sildome faithfull in or wishes [Fol. 1b]
to another mans desires, fare you well. —*Exit*

Ent: Montaigne: Dubois: Longauile. Viramor.

Dubois: here comes yor adversaries brother in lawe

Longa: the lord of *Amiens*

Dubois: from the hall I thinke.

Amie: I did so, saue yor lordship.

Monta: that*es* a wish my lord, as courteous to my present state
as ever honest minde was thankefull for,
for now my safetye must expose it selfe
to question, yet to looke for any free
or hartie salutation (sir from you)
wolld be vnreasonable in me.

Amie: why.

Monta: yor sister is my adversaries wife,
that nearenes needes must consequently drawe
yor Inclination to him.

Amie: I will grante
him all the nearenesse his alliance claymes,
& yet be nothing lesse Impartiall
my lord of *Montaigne*.

Monta: lord of *Montaigne* yet,
but (sir) how long the dignitie or state
belonging to it, will continue, stand*es*
vpon the dangerous passage of this houre,
either for evermore to be confirmd,

47 *Longa:*] *a* altered, ? from *u*   62 *yet*] interlined with a caret

or like the time wherein twas pleaded, gone,
gone wth it, never to be called againe.

Amie: Iustice direct yor processe to the ende,
to both yor persons my respect shall still
be equall, but the righteous cause is that
wch beares my wishes to the side it holdes,
where ever may it prosper. — *Exit*

Mont: then my thankes
are proper to you; yf a man may raise
a confidence vppon a lawfull grounde
I haue no reason to be once perplexed
wth any doubtfull motion: *Longauile*,
that lord of *Amiens* (didst obserue him) has
a worthy nature in him

Longa: Eather tis his nature, or his cunninge.

Mont: thates the vizard of most mens actions, [Fol. 2a]
whose dissembled lives
do carry onely the similitude
of goodnes on em. but for him (*Dubois*)
honest behauior makes a true report
what disposition does Inhabit him,
essentiall vertue,

Long: then tis pitty that
Iniurious *Orleans* is his brother.

Mont: he is but his brother in law.

Long: law, thates as bad.

Dubois: how, is yor law as bad. I rather wish
the hangman thy executor:
then that equiuocation shold be ominous:

Ent:2:Lawiers:— &:2: Creditors:

Long: some of yor lawiers

·1· Law: what is ominous.

·2· Law: let no distrust troble yor lordships thought

84] folio number *(⟨2⟩* above and to the right of this line; folio number *2* added in a modern hand   95 *rather*] *t* altered

·1·*Law:* the Euidences of yor questiond land
haue not so much as any literall
advantage in em to be made against
yor title.

·2·*Law:* and yor counsell vnderstand*es*
the busines fully.

·1·*Law:* theire Industrious, Iust.

·2·*Law:* and very confident.

·1·*Law:* yor state Endures
a voluntary triall. like a man
whose honors are malitiously accusd.

·2·*Law:* the accusation serues to cleare his cause.

·1·*Law:* & to aproue his truth more

·2·*Law:* so shall all
yor adversaries pleading*es*, strengthen yor
possession.

·1·*Law:* & be set vppon recorde,
to witnesse the hereditarie right
of you & yor*es*^.

·2·*Law:* courage. you haue the lawe.

Long: and you the profitt.

Mont: yf discouragement
coo'd worke vpon me, yor assurances
wolld put me strongly into heart agen,
but I was never fearefull, & let *fate*
deceaue my expectation, yet I am
preparde against deiection.

·1·*Credit:* so ar[e] we. [Fol. 2b]

·2·*Credit:* wee haue receiude a comfortable hope
all will speede well:

Long: what is hee *Dubois*:

Dubois: a Creditor.

Long: I thought so, for he speakes
as yf he were a partner in his state,

Mont: sir, I am largely Indebted to yor loues,

Long: more to their purses.

Mont: wch you shall not loose

·1· *Credit:* yor lordship –

Dubois: that*e*s another Creditor

·1· *Credit:* has Interest in me

Long: you haue more of him.

·1· *Credit:* and I haue had so many promises
from these, & all yor learned councellors
how certainlye yor cause will prosper, that

Long-: you brought no seriant*e*s wth you.

Dubois: to attend his Ill successe

Mont: good sir, I will not be
vnthankfull either to theire Industries,
or yor affections

·1· *Law:* all yor lande (my lord)
is at the barr, now, giue me but 10· crownes
Ile saue you harmelesse

Long: take him at his worde.
yf he does loose, yor sau'd by miracell,
for I never knew a lawier yet vndone,

·1· *Law:* then now you shall (sir) yf this prospers not.

Long: sir, I beseech you do not force yor voice
to such a lowdenes, but be thriftie now,
preserue it tell you come to pleade at barr,
It wilbe much more profitable in
the satisfaction then the promise.

·1· *Law:* Is not this a satisfaction, to Engage
my selfe for his assurance.

Dubois yf he dare trust ye.

150 *lande*] *e* altered 151 *crownes*] *n* altered 152 *you*] *o* blotted 153 *his*] *h* blotted

Mont: no sir: my Ruine never shall Import
anothers losse, yf not by accident,
& that my purpose is not guiltye of.
you are Engaged in nothing, but yor care.
attend the *Procurator* to the court.
obserue how thinges Incline, & bringe me worde. *Exit L*⟨ [FOL. 3a]

Long: I dare not sir, yf I be taken there
myne eares will be in danger.

Mont: why? hast thou
cōmitted some thing that deserues thine eares.

Long: no, but I feare the noise, my hearing will be
perished by the noise, & tis as good to want
a member, as to loose the vse,

Mont: the ornament excepted.

Long: well my lord. I'le put em to the hazard. —*Exit Long*

·*1*· *Cred:* yor desires be prosperous to you.

·*2*· *Cred:* or best praiers waite vpon yor fortune. —*Exit Creditors*

Dubois: for yor selues, not him

Mont: thou can'st not blame em, I am in their debtes.

Vera: but had yor large expence (a parte whereof
you owe em) for vnprofitable silkes
& laces, beene bestowed vpon the poore
they wolld haue prayd the right waie, for you,
not vpon you.

Mont: for vnprofitable silkes
& laces. now beleue me honest boy,
th'ast hit vpon a reprehension that belonges
vnto me.

Vera: by my troth (my lord)
I had not so vnmanerly a thought
to reprehend you,

170] folio number ⟨*3*⟩ above and to the right of this line; folio number *3* added in a modern hand   178 *ornament*] *t* written over erased *ed*   180 *desires*] altered, possibly from *desirest*

Mont: why I loue thee for't.
myne owne acknowledgment confirmes thy word*e*s,
for once I do remember, cōming from
the mercers, where my purse had spent it selfe
on those vnprofitable [silks] toyes thou speakest of,
a man halfe naked wth his pouertie
did meete me, & requested my relefe.
I wanted whence to giue it, yet his eyes
spoke for him. those I coo'd haue satisfied
wth some vnfruitfull sorrow. (yf my teares
wolld not haue added rather to his greefe
then easd it, but the true compassion. that
I shold haue giuen I had not, this began
to make me thinke how many such mens wantes
the vaine superfluous cost I wore vpon
my outside, wolld haue cloathed, & left my selfe
a habit as becom̄ing. to Encrease [Fol. 3b]
this new consideration, there came one
clad in a garment plaine & thriftie. yet
as decent as these faire deere follies, made
as yf it weare of purpose to dispise
the vanitie of showe, his purse had still
the powre to doe a charitable deede
& did it.

Dubois: yet yor Inclination sir
deserued no lesse to be cōmended, then his action.

Mont: prethee doe not flatter me,
he that Intend*e*s well, yet depriues himselfe
of meanes to put his good thought into deed*e*s
deceiues his purpose of the dew rewarde
that goodnes meritt*e*s. o antiquitie
thy great examples of nobillitie
are out of Imitation, or at least
so lamelie followd, that thou art as much
before this age in vertue, as in tyme.

205 *sorrow*] ^{1}*o* blotted

Dubois: S^{r}: It must needes be lamely followed. when
the cheefest men that loue to follow it
are for the most part cripples

Mont: who are they

Dubois: soldiors my lord. soldiors,

Mont: tis true, *Duboys*; but yf the law disables me no more
for noble actions? then good purposes.
Ile practise how to exercisse the worth
cōmended to vs by o^{r} auncestors.
the poore neglected soldior shall cōmande
me from a ladyes courtship, & the forme
Ile studye, shall no more be taught me, by
the Tailor, but the scholler, that expence
wch hetherto has beene to Entertaine
th'intemperat pride, & pleasure of the taste
shall fill my table more to satisfie
& lesse to surfet,
what an honeft worke, it wolld be, when we finde
a virgin in her pouerty, & youth
inclyninge to be tempted, to Employ
as much perswasion, and as much expence
to keepe her vpright, as men vse to doe vpon her falling,

Dubois: Tis a charitye that manye maides wilbe vnthankfull for, [Fol. 4a]
& some will rather take it for a wronge,
to by em out of their Inheritance
the thing that they were borne to.

it: Longauile–

Mont: *Longauile*: thou bringest a cherefull promise in thy face,
there standes no pale reporte vpon thy cheeke,
to giue me feare or knowledge of my losse,
tis red, & liuely,

Long: thates wth labor sir; a labor that to those of *Hercules*
may ad another, or (at least) be call'd
an Imitation of his burning shirt,

236 *law*] *aw* altered   253] folio number *(4.* above and to the right of this line

for 'twas a paine of that vnmercifull
perplexitie to shoulder through the thronge
of people that attended yor successe.
my sweatye linnen fixd vpon my skinn
still as they pulld me, tooke that wth it? 'twas
a feare I shold haue left my flesh among em.
It I was patient, for (me thought the toyle
might be an Embleme of the difficult
& wearie passage to get out of law.
& to make vp the deare similitude.
when I was forth seekeing my handkercher,
to wipe my sweat of, I did finde a cause
to make me sweate more, for my purse was lost,
among their fingers.

Dubois: there 'twas rather founde

Long: by them.

Dubois: I meane so.

Mont: well, I will restore
thy damage to thee./how proceedes my sute

Long: like one at brokers, I thinke forfaited.
yor promising councellor at the first
put strongly forward, wth a labourd speede
& such a violence of pleading, that
his fee in sugar candie, scarce will make
his throte a satisfaction for the hurte
he did it, & he carried the whole cause
before him wth so cleare a passage, that
the people in the favor of yor side
cried *Montaigne*, *Montaigne*, in the spight of him
that cryed out silence? & began to laugh
yor adversaries advocate to scorne, [Fol. 4b]
who like a cunning footeman? set me forth
wth such a temperate easie kinde of course
to put him into Exercise of strenght
& follow his advantages so close,
that when yor hot mouthd pleader thought had

270 *toyle*] *o* blotted   284 *at*] interlined with a caret

before he reacht it, he was out of breath, (wun,
& then the other stript him.

Mont: so. all is lost.

Long: but how, I knowe not. for (me thought) I stoode
confounded wth the clamour of the courte
like one Embarqued vpon a storme at sea,
where the tempestious noise of thunder mixte
wth roaringe of the billowes. & the thicke
Imperfect language of the *Sea*=men! takes
his vnderstanding & his safety, both
togeather from him.

Mont: thou dost bring Ill news.

Long: of what I was vnwilling to haue beene
the first reporter.

Mont: didst obserue no more.

Long: at least no better.

Mont: then tha'rt not Inform'd, so well as I am.
I can tell thee that
will please thee, for when all else left my cause,
for my verie adversarye tooke my part.

Long: pox on him, whosoever told you that, abusd you.

Mont: credit me, he tooke my parte
when all forsooke me.

Long: tooke it from you.

Mont: yes, I meane so, & I thinke he had Iust cause
to take it, when the verdict gaue it him;

Dubois: his spirit wolld ha' sunke him, ere he coo'd
haue carried an Ill fortune of this weight, so light.

Mont: nothing is a misery, vnlesse o^{r} weakenesse apprehend it so.
wee cannot be more faithfull to o^{r} selues,
it: the Lawiers in any thing thates manly, then to make
Ill fortune as contemptible to vs.
as it makes vs to others.

308 *men*] altered, ? from *mens*   321 *tooke*] *t* altered, ? from *k*

Long: here come they
whose verie countenances will tell you how
contemptible it is to others. [FOL. 5a]

Mont: Sr.

Long: the sir of knighthood may be giuen em,
ere they heare you now.

Mont: good sir but a word

Dubo: how soone the losse of wealth makes any man
growe out of knowledge

Long: let me see I praye sir;
never stood you vpon the pillorye.

·1· *Law:* the pillorye,

Long: O, now I knowe you did not.
ye aue eares, I thought ye had lost em, pray obserue,
heres one that once was gracious in yor eyes.

·1· *Law:* O my lord,

Long: but haue you nere a counsell, to redeeme
his land yet from the Iudgment.

·2· *Law:* none but this, a writ of error to remoue
the cause.

Long: no more of error, wee haue bin in that to much
alreadye.

·2· *Law:* yf you will reverse the Iudgment, you must trust
to that delaye.

Long: delay (indeed) hees like to trust to that
wth you has any dealing.

·1· *Law:* ere the law procedes to an *habere facias posses
=ionem.*

Dubois: that*e*s a language (sir) I vnderstand not

Long: thart[*e*s] a verie strange vnthankfull fellow,
to haue taken fees of such a liberall measure,
& then giue a man hard word*e*s for's monye.

335] folio number (5. above and to the right of this line   337 *sir*] *i* altered from *a*   350 *his*] *s* blotted

Mont: so, tis gone.

·1· Law: yf men will hazard their salvations,
what shold I saie, I'ue other busines. —*Exit Law.*

Mont: you are ith right.

t: ye Creditors
Ver: I: Rho: that*e*s it you shold saie, now prosperitie has
left me

·1· Cred: haue an eye vpon him, yf wee loose him now,
hees gone for ever, staye & dog him,
Ile go fetch the officers.

Long: dog you him bloodhounde, by this pointe
thou shalt more safelye dog an angrie lyon,
then attempt him.

Mont: whate*s* the matter. [FOL. 5b]

Long: do but stir to fetch a seriant, & besides yor losse
of labour, Ile haue you beaten, tell
those casemente*s* in yor faces be false light*e*s

Dub: falser then those you sell by.

Mont: who gaue you cōmission to abuse my frend*e*s thus,

Long: sir, are those yor frend*e*s that wolld betray you,

Mont: tis to saue themselues, rather then betray me,

·1· Cred yor lordship maks a Iust construction of it,

·2· Cred: all o^{r} desire is but to get o^{r} owne,

Long: yor wives desires and yo^{res} do differ then.

Mont: so far as my habillitie will goe,
you shall haue satisfaction, *Longauile.*

Long: and leaue yor selfe neglected. every man
is first a debtor to his owne demand*e*s, being honest.

Mont: as I take it sir, I did
not Entertaine you for my counsellor.

Long: counsells the office of a servant, when
the m^{r} falls vpon a danger, as
defence is, never threaten wth yor eyes,

386 *owne*] *o* blotted

they are no cockatrices, do you heare
talke wth a girdler, or a milliner
they can Informe you of a kinde of men
that first vndid the profit of those trades
by bringinge vp the forme of carringe
theire *Morglayes* in their hand*e*s; wth some of those
a man maye make himselfe a priuiledge
to aske a question at the prison gates,
wthout yor good permission.

[Both] ·1· *Cred:* by yor leaue

Mont: stay sir, what one example. since the tyme
that first you put yor hat of to me, haue
you noted in me to Incorrage you
to this presumption, by the Iustice now
of thine owne rule, I shold beginne wth thee,
I shold turne thee awaie vngratified,
for all thy former seriuce, & forget
thou ever didst me anye, (sirs) tis not feare
of being arrested, makes me thus Incline
to satisfie you, for you see by him
I lost not all defences wth my state. [Fol. 6a]
the curses of a man, to whome I am
beholding, terrifie me more, then all
the violence he can pursue me wth
Dubois: I did prepare me for the worst,
these 2 small cabinet*e*s do comprehend
the som̄e of all the wealth, that it hath pleasd
adversitye to leaue me, one [es] as rich
as th'other, both in Iewells, take thou this,
& as the order put wthin it, shall
direct thee, distribute it, halfe betweene
those creditors, & th'other halfe among my servant*e*s,
for (sir) they are my creditors,
as well as you are, they haue trusted me
wth their advancement*e*s. yf the value faile
to please you all: my first Increase of meanes
shall offer you a fuller payment, be content

411 *beginne*] ²*e* altered   417] folio number (*6*. above and to the right of this line

to leaue me something, & Imagine that
you put a new beginer into credit.

Creditors: so prosper o^{r} owne blessing*e*s, as wee wish you to yor
(merit

Mont: are yor silences of discontentment, or of sorrow, [*Exe*)]

Dubois: S^{r}: wee wolld not leave you,

Long: do but suffer vs to follow you, & what o^{r} present meanes
or Industries hereafter, can prouide, shall serue you,

Mont O desire me not to liue
to such a basenes, as to be maintained
by those that serue me, pray be gone, I will
defend yor honesties to any man
that shall report you haue forsaken me,
I pray be gone, – why doste thou weepe my boy, – *Exe*
because I do not bid thee goe too. *Cred: seru*

Veramore: no, I weepe (my lord) because I wolld not goe,
I feare you will cōmande me,

Mont: no my childe,
I will not, that wolld discom̄end th'intent
of all my other actions, thou art yet
vnable to advise thy selfe a course,
shold I put thee to seeke it, after that
I must excuse, or at the least forgiue
any vncharitable deede, that can be donne against my selfe,

Ver: Every daye (my lord), I tarrye wth you, Ile accompt
a day of blessing, to me, for I shall
haue so much lesse tyme left me of my life [Fol. 6b]
when I am from you, & yf miserye
befall you, (wch I hope so good a man
was never borne to), I will take my parte,
& make my willingnesse Increase my strenght
to beare it. In the winter I will spare
mine owne clothes from my selfe to couer you,
& in the sommer, carrie some of yo^{res}
to ease you, Ile do any thing I can,

453 *thou*] *t* blotted

Mont: why thou art able to make misery,
ashamed of hurting, when thy weakenes can
both beare it, & despise it, come, my boy
I will prouide some better waye for thee
then this thou speakest of; tis the comfort it,
Ill fortune has vndone me into the fashion,
for now in this age, most men do beginne,
to keepe but one boy, that kept many men —*Exit*

Ent: Orleans *G: Rick:* ***: A Seruant: his Ladye following***

Orle: where is she, call her.

Ladye: I attend you sir.

Orle: yor frend sweete madame,

Ladye: what frend good my lord.

Orle: yo[r]^{r} *Montaigne.* madame, he will shortly want
those courtly graces, that you loue him for.
the meanes where wth he purchast this, & this,
& all his owne prouisions, to the least
proportion of his feeding, or his clothes,
came out of that Inheritance of land,
wch he vniustlye liu'd one, but the law
has giuen me right int, & possession, now
thou shalt perceaue his braueryе vanish, as
this Iewell does from thee now, & these pearles
to him that owes em.

Ladye: you are the owner sir,
of everye thing that does belong to me.

Orle: no, not of him sweet ladye.

Ladye: O good heaven,

Orle: but in a while yor minde will change, & bee
as readye to disclaime him, when his wantes
& miseries haue perishd his good face
& taken of the sweetnesse, that has made
him pleasing in a womans vnderstanding, [FOL. 7a]

477 *G: Rick:*] interlined with a caret 501] folio number (7 above and to the right of this line

Ladye: O heaven, how gracious had creation beene
to woemen, who are borne wthout defence
yf to or hart*e*s there had beene doores, through wch
or husband*e*s might haue look't into or thought*e*s,
& made themselues vndoubtfull.

Orle: made em mad

Ladye: wth honest women

Orle: thou dost still pretend
a title to that vertue, prethee let
thy honestie speake freelye to me now,
thou knowest that *Montaigne*, of whose land
I am the mr, did affect thee first,
& shold haue had thee, yf the strenght of frend*e*s
had not preuaild aboue thine owne consent,
I haue vndone him, tell me how thou doest
consider his Ill fortune, & my good.

Ladye: Ile tell you Iustly, his vndoinge is
an argument for pittye? & for teares,
in all theire dispositions that haue knowne
the honor & the goodnes of his life,
yet that addition of prosperitye
wch you haue got by't, no Indifferent man,
will malice or repine at, yf the law
be not abusd in't, howsoever, since
you haue the vpper fortune of him, 'twill
be some dishonor to you, to beare yor selfe
wth anye pride or glorie over him.

Orle: this may be truly spoken, but in thee
it is not honest.

Ladye: yes, so honest,
t: Amiens: — that I care not yf the chast *Penelope*
weare now alive to heare me

Orle: who comes there.

Lady: my brother.

528 *anye*] *y* altered from *i*

Amie: saue ye.

Orle: now sir,
you haue hearde of prosperous *Montaigne.*

Amie: no sir, I haue heard of *Montaigne*,
but of yor prosperitie

Orle: Is he distracted

Amie: he does beare his losse
wth such a noble strenght of patience, that
had fortune eyes to see him: she wolld weepe [FOL. 7b]
for hauinge hurt him, & pretendinge that
she did it but for triall of his worth
hereafter ever loue him,

Orle: I perceaue you loue him; & because (I must confesse)
he does deserue it, though for some respect*e*s
I haue not giuen him that acknowledgment,
yet in myne honor; I did still conclude to vse him noblie,

Amie: S^{r}, it will become yor reputation,
& make me growe prowde of yor alliance,

Orle: I did reserue the doinge of this frendship
tell I had his fortunes at my mercye,
that the world may tell him tis a willing curtesie,

Ladye: this change will make me happie

Orle: tis a change,
thou shalt behold it, then obserue me,
that *Montaigne* had possession of my land,
I was his riuall, & at last obtaynd
this ladye, who by promise of her owne
affection to him, shold haue beene his wife,
I had her, & wth held her like a pawne,
tell now my land is renderd to me agen,
& since it is so, you shall see, I haue
the conscience not to keepe her, giue him her,
for by the ffaithfull temper of my sword.
she shall not tarrie wth me. } drawes. /

548 *because*] *se* altered 555 *at*] *t* written over an erasure.

Amie: giue me waye, — } *drawes.*
thou most vnworthie man, death giue me waie,
or by the wronge he does thy Innocence,
Ile end thy miserye, & his wickednes togeather,

Ladye: staye, & let me Iustefie
my husband in it, — I haue wrongd his bed, – } *Exit*
never. all shames that can afflict me, fall } *Amiens*
vpon me, yf I ever wrongd you.

Orle: didst thou not confesse it

Ladye: 'twas to saue yor blood from shedinge,
It has turnd my brothers edge,
he that beholdes o^{r} thoughtes as plainlye as
o^{r} faces, knowes that I did never hurte
my honestie but by accusinge it,

Orle: womens consentes are sooner credited
it:2: Seruants then theire denialls, & Ile never trust
Rick: her bodye that preferres anye defence
before the safetie of hir honor. — here [Fol. 8a]
showe forth that stranger. — giue me not a worde,
thou seest a danger readye to be tempted,

Ladye: caste that vpon me, rather then my shame,
& as I am a dyinge, I will vowe
that I am honest,

Orle: put her out of dores,
but that I feare my land may goe againe
to *Montaigne*. I wolld kill thee, I am loath
to make a begger of him that waie, or else, —
goe, now you haue the libertie of flesh.
& you may put it to a dooble vse,
one for yor pleasure, th'other to maintaine
yor well beloued. he will be in wante,
In such a charitable exercise,
the vertue will excuse you for the vice, — *Exeunt*

587] folio number *(·8·* above and to the right of this line

Ent: Amiens: At one doore: Montaigne: and Veramour. At Another:

Mont: what meanes yor lordship, — } *they drawe:*

Vera: ffor the loue of heaven,

Amie: thou hast advantage of me, cast awaie that buckler,

Mont: so he is sir, for he liues
wth one that is vndone, avoide vs boy.

Ver: Ile first avoide my safetye,
yor rapier shall be buttond wth my head,
before it touch my m^{r}.

Amie: *Montaigne*?

Mont: sir,

Amie: you know my sister.

Mont: yes sir.

Amie: for a whore. — **_Ent: the Ladye Orleans:_**

Mont: you lye, & shall lye lower, yf you dare abuse hir honor.

Ladye: I am honest.

Amie: honest?

Ladye: vpon my faith I am.

Amie: what did then perswade thee to condemne thy selfe.

Ladye: yor safetye,

Amie: I had rather be exposd
to danger then dishonor, th'ast betraid
the reputation of my familie
more baselye by the falsenes of that worde
then yf thou hadst deliuerd me a sleepe [FOL. 8b]
into the hand*e*s of a base Enimie,
releife will never make thee sensible
of thy disgraces, let thy want*e*s compell thee to it.
—*Exit Amiens*

Ladye: O, I am a miserable woeman.

606 *ffor*] ^{1}f written over erasure 607 *that*] altered from *this*

Mont: why maddam, are you vtterly wthout meanes
to releiue you.

Ladye: I haue nothing sir,
vnlesse by changing of these clothes for worse,
& then at last the worst for nakednesse.

Mont: stande of boy. nakednes wolld be a change
to please vs madame, to delight vs both.

Ladye: what nakednes, sir.

Mont: why, the nakednes of bodye madame,
wee were louers once.

Ladye: never dishonest louers.

Mont: honestie has no allowance now to giue o^{r}selues,

Ladye: nor you allowance against honestie,

Mont: Ile send my boy hence, opportunitie
shalbee o^{r} servant, come, & meete me first,
wth kisses like a stranger, at the dore,
& then Invite me neerer to receaue
a more familliar Inwarde wellcome, where
Insteede of tapers made of virgine wax
th'increasinge flames of o^{r} desires shall light
vs to a banquet, & before the taste
be dull wth satisfaction, Ile prepare
a nourishment composd of every thing
that beares a naturall frendship to the blood.
& that shall set another hedge vppont,
or else betweene the courses of the ffeast
wee'le dalye out an exercise of tyme
that ever as one appetite expires,
another may succede it,

Ladye: O my lord.
how has yor nature lost her worthinesse.
when o^{r} affections had theire libertye,
o^{r} kisses met as temperatlye as
the hand*es* of [brothers] sisters, or of brothers, yet
o^{r} blood*es* were then as mouing, then you weare

634 *are*] *r* blotted   636 *nothing*] *o* altered   667 *yet*] *y* altered, possibly from *I*

so noble, that I durste haue trusted your
Embraces in an opportunitie
silent ynough to serue a rauisher,
and yet come from you vndishonord, how [FOL. 9a]
you thinke me alterd, that you promise yor
attempt successe, I knowe not, but were all
the sweet temptations that deceiue vs, set
on this side, & on that side all the wants,
these neather shold perswade me, nor they force.

Mont: then missery may waste yor bodye.

Ladye: yes, but lust shall never.

Mont: I haue founde you still
as vncorrupted as I left you first,
continew so, & I will serue you w^th
as much deuotion as my worde, my hande
or purse can showe you, & to Iustefie
that promise. here is halfe the wealth I haue,
take it, you owe me nothing tell you fall
from vertue, wch the better to protect,
I haue bethought me of a present meanes.
giue me the letter, — this cōmend*es* my boy
into the seruice of a ladye, whose
free goodnes you haue bin aquainted w^th. *Lamira*.

Ladye: sir, I knowe her

Mont: then beleiue her Entertainement wilbe noble to you.
my boy shall bringe you thether, & relate
yor manner of misfortune, so, I kisse yor hand
good ladye.

Ladye: S^r: I knowe not how to promise,
but I cannot be vnthankfull.

Mont: all that you can Imploye in thanckfullnes,
be yo^res. to make you the more prosperous.
farewell my boy, I am not yet oppressd.
haueing the powre to helpe one that*es* distressd.

672] folio number *(·9·* above and to the right of this line *yet*] *y* written over erasure

Exeunt

Actus: Secundj: Scæna: Pri:

Ent: Longauile: And Dubois:

Long: what shall wee do now, sword*es* are out of vse,
& word*es* are out of credit,

Dubois: wee must serue,

Long: the meanes to get a seruice will first spend
o^{r} purses, & except wee can allow
o^{r} selues an Entertainement, seruice will
neglect vs, now tis growne into a doubt [Fol. 9b]
whether the m^{r} or the servant giues the countenance;

Dub: then fall in wth m^{rs}.es.

Long: they keepe more servant*es* now (indeede) then men,
but yet the age is growne so populous,
of those attendant*es*, that the women are
growne full to.

Dub: what shall wee propounde o^{r} selues.

Long: Ile thinke on't.

Dub: do, olde occupations haue to many setters vp,
to prosper, some vncōmon trade wolld thriue now.

Long: [wee'le Ene make vp some halfe a dozen proper men,
& set vp a male stewes, wee shold get more
then all yor female sinners]

Dub: [yf the house be seated as It shold be priuatlye,]

Long: [I, but that wolld make a multitude of witches]

Dub: [witches, how I prethee.]

Long: [thus, the bawdes wolld all turne witches, to revenge
themselues vpon vs, & the women that
came to vs, for disguises must weare beardes,
& that*es* they saie the token of a witch,]

Dub: [what shall wee then doe.]

Long: [wee must studie on't wth more consideration,]
staie *Dubois*; is not the lord of *Orleans*
& the lord of *Amiens* Enimyes.

735 *is*] *s* altered

Dub: yes, what of that,

Long: me thinkes the ffactions of two such great men
shold giue a promise of [advantage] advancement now,
to vs that want it,

Dub: let the plot be thine, & In the Enterprize Ile second
(thee,

Long: I haue it, wee will first set downe o^{r} selues,
the method of a quarrell, & make choice
of some frequented taverne, or such a place
of com̄on notice to performe it in,
by waie of vndertakeing to maintaine
the severall honors of those Enimyes,
thou for the lord of *Orleans*, I for *Amiens*.

Dub: I like the proiect, & I thinke 'twill take
the better, since their difference first did rise[,]
from his occasion whome we followd once,

Long: wee cannot hope lesse after the reporte
then Entertainement or gratuitie,
yet those are end*e*s I do not aime at most,
great spiritt*e*s that are needye, & will thriue
must labor, whilest such trobles are aliue, [FOL. 10a]
— Exe

Ent: Lauerduer: And Captaine Lapoop:

Lapoop: hunger is sharper then the sword, I haue fed this
three dayes vpon leafe tobacco, for want of other

Lauer: you haue liu'd the honester Captaine, (victualls.
but be not so deiected. but hold vp thy head, & meate
will sooner fall i'thy mouth,

Lapoop: I care not so much for meate, yf I had but good
liquor, for wch my gutt*e*s croake like so many frogg*e*s
for raine

Lauer: It seemes you are trobled wth the winde collick,
yf you be Captaine swallow a bullet, tis present
remedye Ile assure you.

757] folio number *(10.* above and to the right of this line 759 *Lauerduer*] *er* altered from *re*

Lapoop: a bullet! why man my panch is nothing but a pile
of bullet*e*s, when I was in any seruice, I stoode betwene
my generall & the shot, like a mud wall. I am all
lead from the Crowne of the head to the sole of the
ffoote, not a sound bone about me,

Lauer: It seemes you haue beene in terrible hot seruice
Captaine

Lapoop: It has ever beene the [fall.e] fault of the low countrye
warres, to spoile many a man. I ha' not bin the
first nor shall not be the last, but Ile tell you
sir, (hunger has brought it into minde) I serued
once at the seige of *Brest*, tis memorable to this
daye, where wee were in great distresse for victualls,
whole troopes fainted, more for wante of foode, then
for blood, & dyed, yet wee were resolu'd to stand
it out, I my selfe was but then gent of a companye,
& had as much neede as anye man, & Indeed I
had perishd had not a miraculous prouidence
preseru'd me.

Lauer: as how good Captaine

Lapoop: marry sir Ene as I was faintinge, & falling downe
for want of sustainance, the Enemie made a shot at
me, & struck me full ith paunch wth a penye loafe.

Lauer: Insteed of a bullet.

Lapoop: Insteed of a bullet.

Lauer: that was miraculous indeede, & that loafe sustaind you,

Lapoop: nourished me, or I had famishd wth the rest,

Lauer: you haue done worthy Act*e*s being a soldior, & now [FOL. 10b]
you shall giue me leaue to requite yor tale, &
to aquainte you wth the most notorious deedes
that I haue done being a Courtier, I protest Captaine
I will lye no more then you haue done,

Lapoop: I can Indure no lyes.

778 *fault*] interlined with a caret

Lauer: I knowe you cannot Captaine, therefore Ile only tell you of strange thing*es*. I did once a deede of charitye for it selfe; I assisted a poore widdow in a sute, & obtained it, & yet I protest I tooke not a penye for my labor.

Lapoop: this is no such strange thing.

Lauer: by *Mars* Captaine, but it is, [& a verie strange thinge to in a Courtier,] It may take the vpper hande of yor penye loafe for a miracle. I coo'd haue tolde you how manye ladyes haue languished for my loue, and how I was once solicited by the mother, the daughter, & grandmother, out of the least. I might haue diggd my selfe a fortune, they were all great ladyes. for two of em weare so big, I coo'd hardlye Embrace them, but I was sluggish in my rising courses & therefore let them passe, what meanes I had, is spent vpon such as had the wit to cheate me, that

Ent: Montagne: – And Maly=corne

wealth being gone, I haue only bought experience wth it, wth a stronge hope to cheate others, — but see, here comes the much declyned *Montagne*, who had all his mannor houses wch weare the bodye of his estate, ouerthrowne by a great winde,

Lapoop: how, by a great winde? was he not overthrowne by

Lauer: yes marry was he, but there was terrible puffing (law & blowing before he was overthrowne, yf you obserud, & beleue it Captaine, theres no winde so dangerous to ruine a building, as a lawiers breath.

Lapoop: whate*s* hee wth him

Lauer: an Eminent Cittizen, *Monsier Malycorne*, lete*s* stand aside, & listen their designes.

Maly: S^{r}: proffit is the crowne of labour, It is the life, the soule of the Industrious marchant, in it he makes his parradise, & for It neglecte*s* wife, children, frende*s*, parente*s*, nay all the world, & deliuers vp himselfe to the violence of stormes, & to be tossd into vnknowne

830 *ruine*] interlined with a caret   831 *hee*] [2]*e* added over erasure affecting *w* in *wth*

[Fol. 11a]

ayers; as there is no ffacultye so perilous, so there is none so worthy proffitable.

Mont: Sr: I am verie well possest of it, & what of my poore fortunes remaines, I wolld gladlye hazard vpon the sea. It cannot deale worse wth me then the land, though It sincke or throwe it into the hand*es* of pirat*es*. I haue yet 500 pound*es* left, & yor honest & worthy aquaintance may make me a yonge marchant the one moytye of what I haue, I wolld gladlye adventer.

Maly: how, adventer, you shall hazard nothing, you shall only Ioine wth me in certaine Cōmodityes that are safe arriued vnto the key, you shall neither be in doubt of danger nor damage, but so much monye disburste, so much receau'd, sir, I wolld haue you conceaue I pursue it not for anye good yor monye will do me, but meerly out of myne owne freenes & curtesie to pleasure you.

Mont: I can beleeue no lesse, & you expresse a noble nature, seekinge to build vp a man so ruind as my (selfe.

Lauer: Captaine, here is subiect for vs to worke vpon yf wee haue wit, you here that there is monye yet left, & It is going to be layd out in rattells, bells, hobby horses, or browne paper, some such like sale cōmodityes, now It wolld do better in or purses, or vppon or back*es* in good gold lace & scarlet, & then wee might pursue or proiect*es* & or deuices toward*es* my ladye *Lamira*, goe to, theres a conceite newly landed, harke. I stand in good reputation wth him, & therefore may the better cheate him; Captaine, take a few Instructions from me.

Mont: what monyes I haue is at yor disposing, & vppon 12· I will meete you at the pallace wth it,

839] folio number *(11* above and to the right of this line *ayers*] *s* blotted 846 *marchant*] *t* interlined with a caret 853 *disburste*] [2]*s* blotted 862 *hobby*] *h* written over dot 864 *backes*] written below an erasure

Maly: I will there expecte you, & so I take my leaue, — *Exit*

Lauer: you apprehend me,

Lapoop: why doe you thinke I am a dunce.

Lauer: not a dunce Captaine, but you might giue me leaue to misdoubt that pregnancye in a soldior, wch is proper & hereditarye to a Courtier, but prosecute it, I will both second & giue credit to it, — good *Monsir Montagne*, I wolld yor whole revenewes laye wthin the circuite of myne armes, that I might as easilye bestowe [Fol. 11b] it or restore it vnto you as my curtesie.

Lapoop: my zealous wishes, sir, do accompanie his for yor good fortune.

Lauer: beleiue it sir, or affection towardes you is a stronge bande of frendship.

Mont: to wch I shall most willingly seale, – but beleeue it gent, in a broken estate, the bond of frendship [is] oft is forfetted, but that it is yor free and Ingenious natures to renew it.

Lauer: Sr: I will amplye extend my selfe to yor vse, & am very zealously afflicted as not one of yor least frendes for yor crooked *fate*, but let it not cease you wth anye deiection, you haue as I here a sufficient competen =cye left, wch well disposed may erect you as high in the worldes accompt as ever.

Mont: I cannot liue to hope it, much lesse Inioye it, nor is it any part of my Endeavor, my studye is to render every man his owne, & to containe my selfe wthin the limittes of a gent.

Lauer: I haue the grante of an office giuen me by some noble fauorites of myne in courte. there standes but a small matter betweene me & it; yf yor abillitie be such to lay downe the present some; out of the loue I beare you, before any other man, It shalbe confirmd yores.

Mont: I haue heard you often speake of such a thing, yf it be assurd to [me] you: I [wolld] will gladly deale in it, that portion I haue I wolld not hazard vppon an vnknowne course, for I see the most certainest is Incertaintye

Lapoop: hauinge monye sir, you could not light vpon men that could giue you better direction, there is at this tyme, a frend of myne vpon the seas, to be plaine wth you, he is a pirate, that hath writ to me to worke his freedome, & by this gentlemans meanes whose aquaintance Is not small at court, wee haue the worde of a worthy man for it, only there is some monye to bee suddenly disbursd, & if yor happinesse be such to make it vp. you shall receaue treble gaine by it, & good assurance for it.

Mont: gent, out of the weakenesse of my estate. you seeme to haue some knowledge of my brest, that wolld yf it [Fol. 12a] were possible advance my declined fortunes, to satisfie all men of whome I haue had credit, & I knowe no waie better then theise wch you propose. I haue some monye readye vnder my cōmande, some parte of it is all readye promisd, but the remainer is yores, to such vses as are propounded.

Lauer: appointe some certaine place of meeting, for these affaires require expedition,

Mont: I will make it my present busines, at 12· I am to meete *Monsir Malycorne* the marchant, at the pallace, you knowe him sir, about some negotiation of the same nature, there I will be readye to tender you that monye vpon such conditions as wee shall conclude of,

Lauer: the care of it be yores, so much as the affaire concernes you,

Mont: yor Caution is effectuall, tell then I take my leaue, – *Exit*

Lauer: good *Monsir Montagne*.

914 *me*] *m* begun as *w* 922] folio number *(12.* above and to the right of this line 925 *theise*] altered from *those*
933 *you*] *o* blotted

Wthin: *Clashing of weapons: some crying downe wth theire weapons: then Enter Longauile: Dubois: their Swords drawne: 3: or: 4:* [*Seruantes*] *Drawers betwene Em:*

Seru: nay gent, what meane you, pray be quiet, haue some
respect vnto the house

Long: a treacherous slaue

Dubo: thou dost revile thy selfe, base *Longauile.*

Long: I say thou art a villaine, & a corrupt one,
that hast some 7· yeares fed on thy masters trencher,
yet never bredst good blood towardes him, for yf thou
hadst, thow'dst haue a sounder harte.

Dub: so sir. you can vse yor tongue some thing nimblier then
yor sword

Long: wolld you could vse yor tongue well of yor masters frend.
you might haue better Emploiement for yor sword.

Dub: I saie agen. & I will speake it lowde & often,
that *Orleans* is a noble gent, wth whome
Amiens is to light to poise the skale.

Long: he is the weaker for takinge of a praise
out of thy mouth.

Dub: this hande shall seale his merit at thy harte.

Lauer: parte them my masters, parte them.

Seru: parte em sir, why doe not you parte em, you stand by wth
yor sworde in yor hande, & cry parte em.

Lauer: why you must knowe my frend, my clothes are [FOL. 12b]
better then yo^{res}, & in a good sute I do never vse
to part anyebodye,

Lapoop: and It is discretion,

Lauer: I marry is it Captaine

Long: *Dubois*, though this place priuiledge thee,
knowe where next wee meete,

941 *Drawers*] interlined with a caret 954 *haue*] *h* written over erased *b* 965 *do*] *d* altered.

the blood wch at thy harte flowes, drops at thy feete,

t: Amiens: *Dub:* I wolld not spend it better then in this quarrell.
sword drawne & on such a hazard.

Amie: what vprores this! must my name here be questiond.
In taverne brawles, & by affected ruffins?

Lauer: not wee indeede sir.

Dub: ffeare cannot make me shrinke out of yor ffurie,
though you weare greater then yor name doth make you.
I am one &, the opposer. yf yor swolne rage
haue ought in mallice to Inforce, expresse it,

Amie: I seeke thee not, nor shalt thou ever gaine
that credit wch a blowe from me wold giue thee,
by my blood. I more detest that fellow
wch tooke my parte, then thee, that he durste offer
to take my honor in his feeble armes,
& spend it in a drincking roome. wch way went he,

Lauer: that waie sir, I wolld you wolld after him
for I do feare wee shall haue more scufflinge,

Amie: Ile follow him. & yf my speede ore take him,
I shall Ill thanke him for his forwardnes. *Exit*

Lauer: I am glad hees gone, for I do not loue to see a
sword drawne in the hand*es* of a man that looks so
furious. theres no Iesting wth edge tooles, how
t: Orleans: — say you Captaine.

Lapo: I say tis better Iesting, then to be in earnest wth them.

Orle: how now, whate*s* the difference, they saie there haue
beene sworde*s* drawne, & in my quarrell; let me
knowe that man whose loue is so sincere
to spend his blood for my sake, I will bounteouslye
requite him.

Lauer: wee were all of yor side, but there he stande*s* began it,

Orle: whate*s* thy name,

Du: *Dubois.*

973 *hazard*] *h* written over erasure   979 &] interlined with a caret   998 *sincere*] *s* altered

Orle: giue me thy hande! thou hast receau'd no hurt,

Du: not any? nor were this bodye stuck full of wound*e*s,
I shold not counte them hurtes, being taken
in so honorable a cause, as the defence [FOL. 13a]
of my most worthy lord.

Orle: the dedication of thy loue to me,
requires my ample bountye, thou art myne,
for I do finde thee made vnto my purposes,
Monsir Lauerdure, pardon my neglect[,]
I not obserud you, and how runs rumor,

Lauer: why It runnes my lord like a footeman wthout a cloake,
to showe that what once is rumord cannot be hid,

Orle: & what saies the rable, am not I the subiect of their
talke.

Lauer: troth my lord. the cōmon mouth speakes fowle word*e*s.

Orle: of me, for turninge awaie my wife, do they not,

Lauer: faith the men do a little murmer at it, & saie, tis an Ill
president, in so great a man, marry, the woemen they
raile out right.

Orle: out vpon them rampallions: Ile keepe my selfe safe
Enough out of their fingers, but what saie my pretye
Idlye composed gallant*e*s, that censure every thing more
desperatlye then it is dangerous; what say they.

Lauer: marry they are layeing wagers what death you shall
dye, one offerd to laye 500.li & yet he had but a groate
about him. & that was in too toopences too, to anye man
that wolld make it vp a shilling, that you were
killd wth a pistoll chargd wth white powder. another
offerd to pawne his soule for 5.s & yet no bodye
wolld take him, that you were stab'd to death. and
shold dye wth more woundes then *Cæsar*.

Orle: and who shold be the *Brutus* that shold do it,
Montagne. and his associat*e*s.

Lauer: so tis coniecturd.

1007] folio number *(13.* above and to the right of this line 1035 *who*] interlined with a caret

Lapoop: & beleeue it sweete prince it is to be feared, & therefore
prevented.

Orle: by turninge his purpose on himselfe, were not that the

Lauer: the most direct path for yor safetye. (waie.
for where doth danger sit more furious, then in a desperat ma⟨n⟩

Lapoop: and being you haue declined his meanes, you haue
Increased his mallice.

Lauer: besides the generall reporte that steemes in everye mans
breath, & staines you all over wth Infamye, that *Tyme*
the devourer of all thing*e*s cannot eate out.

Lapoop: I, for that former familiaritye, wch he had wth yor ladye.

Lauer: men speake it as boldlye as word*e*s of complement, [Fol. 13b]
good morrow, good even, or god saue you sir, are not
more vsuall, yf the verie word cuckold had beene
written vpon yor forhead in great Capitall letters.
It coo'd not haue beene dilated wth more confidence.

Orle: he shall not sleepe another night, I will haue his blood,
though it be required at my hand*e*s agen.

Lauer: yor lordship maye, & wthout hazarding yor owne person,
heres a gent in whose looks I see a resolution to
performe it.

Du: let his lordship giue me but his honorable word
for my safetye. Ile kill him as hee walkes.

Lauer: or pistoll him as he sit*e*s at meate

Lapoo: or at game.

Lauer: or as he is drincking.

Du: any waie.

Orle: willt thou? call what is myne thine owne,
thy reputation shall not be brought in question
for it, much lesse thy life, it shall be namde
a deede of valour in thee, not murder. farewell.
—*Exit*

Du: I neede no more Encouragement. It is a worke
I will perswade my selfe that I was borne to

Lauer: and you may perswade yor selfe to that you shall
merit by it, being that it is for his honorable
lordship.

Du: but you must yeild me meanes, how, when, & where.

Lauer: that shalbee or taskes, nay more. wee wilbe agent*es* wth
this houre wee are to meete him, on the receite (thee.
of certaine monyes, wch Indede wee purpose honestlye
to cheate him of,
& that*es* the maine cause I wolld haue him slaine,
who works wth safetye, makes a double gaine.
—— *Exeunt*

Ent: Longauile: Amience following him,

Amie: staye sir, I haue tooke some paines to overtake you.
yor name is *Longauile.*

Long: I haue the word of manye honest men for't. I craue
yr lordships pardon, yor sodaine apprehension of my
stepes, made me to frame an answer vnwitting and
worthy yor respect

Amie: do you knowe me.

Long: yes my lord

Amie: I knowe not you, nor am I well pleasd to make this [Fol. 14a]
time as the affaire stand*es* the Induction of yor aquaint
=ance, you are a fighting ffellowe

Long: how my lord.

Amie: I thinke I to much grace you, rather you are a fellow
dare not fight, but spitt & puffe, & make a noise,
whilste yor trembling hande drawes out yor sword,
to try it vpon andirons, stooles, or tables, rather then
[of] on a man.

Long: yor honor may best speake this, yet by my life wth litle
safetie yf I thought it serious.

Amie: come, you are a mere bragart, & you haue giuen me
cause to tell you so, what weakenes haue you ever
seene in me, to prompt yor selfe that I shold neede

1078 *honestlye*] 1*e* written over erased letter 1092] folio number (*14* above and to the right of this line

yor helpe, or what other reason coo'd Induce you too't.
you never had a meales meate from my table, nor as
I remember from my wardrobe any cast sute.

Long: tis true. I never durste yet haue such a seruile sperit,
to be the minion of a full swolne lord, but alwaies
did detest such slauery, a meales meate! or a cast
sute! I wolld first eate the stones, & from such ragg*e*s the
dunghills does afford, pick me a garment.

Amie: I haue mistooke the man, his resolute spirit
proclaymes him generous he has a noble harte
as free to vtter good deedes as to act them.
for had he not beene right, & of one peece,
he wolld haue crumpled, curled, & shrunck himselfe
out of the shape of man into a shadowe.
but prethee tell me, yf no such fawninge hope
did leade thee on to hazard life for my sake.
what was it that Incited thee, tell me,
speake it wthout the Imputation of a *Sicophant*.

Long: yor owne desert,
& wth it was Ioined the vnfaigned frendship
that I Iudgd you ever held vnto my former lord,

Amie: the noble *Montagne*.

Long: yes, the noble, & much Iniurd *Montagne*.

Amie: to such a man as thou art my hart shalbe a casket,
I will lock thee vp there, & esteeme thee
as a faithfull frend, the richest Iewell
that a man Inioyes. & being thou didst follow once my frend.
& in thy harte still doste, not wth his fortunes casting him of,
thou shalt go hande in hande wth me, & share
as well in my abillitie, as loue, tis not my end,
to gaine men for my vse, but a true frend. — *Exeunt*

t: Dubois—

Dub: theres no such thriuing waie to liue in grace [Fol. 14b]
as to haue no sence of it, his [bac] back nor belly
shall not want warminge that can practise mischefe,
I walke now wth a full purse, growe high, & wanton,

1138 *no*] interlined with a caret *back*] *k* altered, possibly from *ll* 1139 *warminge*] *m* altered

prune, & baske my selfe in the bright shine
of his good lordhips fauors, & for what vertue,
for fashioning my selfe a murderer.
O noble *Montagne*, to whome I owe my harte,
wth all my best thought*e*s, tho' my tongue haue promisd
to exceede the mallice of thy destenie,
never in time of all my seruice, knew I
such a sin tempt thy bountye. those that did feede
vpon thy charge. had merit, or else neede,

Ent: Lauerdure: & Lapoope: wth/ disguises/

Lau: Dubois: most prosperouslye met,

Du: how now, will he come this waye,

/ *Lau:* this waie, Im̄ediatlye, therefore thy assistance. deare (*Duboys*.

Du: what, haue you cheated him of the monye you spoke of.

Lauer: phue, as easilye as a sillye countrye wench of her maidenhead, wee had it in a twinckling.

Du: tis well, Captaine let me helpe you, you must be or leader in this action.

Lapoop: tut, feare not, Ile warrante you if my sword hold weele make no sweating busines of it,

Du: why that*e*s well said, but let*e*s retire a litle, that wee may come on the more brauely, this waie. this waie

— *Exeunt*

Ent: Montagne: 3: Officers: 3: Creditors:

·1· Cred: officers, looke to him, & be sure you take good securitye, before hee parte from you.

Mont: why but, my frend*e*s, you take a strange course wth me. the som̄es I owe you are rather forgetfullnes, they are so slight, then wante of will or honestie to pay you.

·1· Cred: I sir, It may be so, but wee must be paid, & wee will be paide, before you scape. wee haue wife and children, & a charge, & you are goinge downe the winde as a man maye saie, & therefore it behooues vs to looke too't in tyme.

1168 *they ... slight,*] interlined with a caret   1171 *wife*] *f* altered

·2· Cred: yor Cloake here wolld satisfie me, mynes not aboue
3·li matter, besides the arrest.

·3· Cred: ffaith, & myne is much about that matter, too; yor girdle and
hangers, & beauer, shalbe sufficient bayle for't.

·1· Cred: yf you haue ever a plaine black sute at home, this
wth yor silke stockinges, garters & roses, shall pacifye me
too, for I take no delight yf I haue a sufficient pawne,
to cast anye gent in prison, therefore tis but an [FOL. 15a]
vntrussing matter, & you are free, wee are no vnreason=
able creatures you see, for myne owne parte I
protest I am loath to put you to any trouble, but
for securitye.

Mont: Is there no more of you. he wolld next demaund my skin.

·1· Cred: no sir, heres no more of [you,] vs, nor do anye of vs demaund
yor skin, wee knowe not what to doe wth't, but it may bee
yf you owed yor glouer any monye, he knewe, what
vse to make of it.

Mont: ye dregges of basenes, vultures amongst men,
ıt: Malycorne] that tyer vpon the hartes of generous spirittes,

·1· Cred: you do vs wronge sir, wee tyre no generous spirittes,
t: Malycorne:—wee tyre nothing but or hacknyes.

Mont: but here comes one made of another peece.
a man well meriting that free borne name
of Cittizen, wellcome my deliuerer, I am falne
into the handes of bloodhoundes, that for a so͞me
lesser then theire honesties, wch is nothinge,
wolld teare me out of my skin.

Maly: why sir, whates the matter.

·1· Cred: why sir, the matter is that wee must haue or monye, wch
yf wee cannot haue, wee'le satisfye or selues wth his
carcasse, & be paide that waies. you had as good sir
you had not beene so peremptorye. officers. hold fast.

·1· Officer: the strenuous fist of vengance now is clutcht, there
fore feare nothing.

1182] folio number *(15* above and to the right of this line 1183 *you*] altered, ? from *y'art* or *y'rt* 1205 *paide*] *a* altered, possibly from *e*

Maly: what may be the debt In grosse.

Mont: some fortye crownes, nay rather not so much, tis quickly (cast

Maly: tis strange to me that yor estate shold haue so lowe an eb, to stick at such slight som̄es. why my frend*es* you are to strict in yor accompt*es*, & call to sodaine on this g̅e̅n̅t̅, he has hopes yet left to paie you all.

·*1*· *Cred:* hopes! I marry, pray bid him pay his frend*es* wth his hopes, & pay vs wth currant coyne, I knewe a [gallant] gallant once that fed his creditors still wth hopes, and bid em they shold feare nothing, for he had em tyed in a stringe, & trust me so he had indeede, for at last he & all his hopes hopte in a halter.

Mont: good sir, wth what speede you maye free me out of the companye of these slaues, that haue nothing but theire names to showe em men.

Maly: what wolld you wish me doe sir; I protest I ha'not [Fol. 15b] the present som̄e (small as it is) to lay downe for you, & for giuing my word, my frend*es* no later then yester =night. made me take bread & eate it, that I shold not doe it for any man breathing ith world, therefore I pray hold me excusde,

Mont: you doe not speake this seriouslye.

Maly: as ever I said my praiers I protest to you.

Mont: what may I thinke of this.

Maly: troth sir. thought is free, for any man, wee abuse o^{r} betters in it, I haue done it my selfe

Mont: trust me this speech of yo^{res} doth much amaze me, pray leaue this language, & out of that same som̄e you latelye did receaue of me, laye downe as much as may discharge me.

Maly: you are a merrie man sir, & I am glad you take yor crosses so temperatlye. fare you well sir: – & yet I haue

1213 *stick*] *s* altered from *I*

some thing more to saie to you, a worde in yor eare I pray, to be plaine wth you, I did laye this plot to arrest ye, to Inioye the [this] monye I haue of yores, wth the more safetye. I am a foole to tell you this now, but in good faith I coo'd not keepe it in, & the monye wolld haue done me litle good else, an honest Cittizen cannot wholye Inioye his owne wife for you, they growe olde before they haue the true vse of em, wch is a lamentable thing, & truly much hardens the hart*e*s of vs Cittizens against you. I can saie no more, but am hartelye sorrie for yor heavinesse, & so I take my leaue. ———*Exit*

·I· Cred: officers, laye hold on him agen, for *Monsir Malycorne* will do nothing for him I perceaue,

t: Dubois –
poop: Lauerdure/ *Du:* nay, come on my masters, leaue dancing the old measures, /and let*e*s assault him bravelye.

Lauer: by no meanes, for It goes against my stomack. to kill a man in an vniust quarrell.

Lapoop: It must needes be a clog to his conscience all his life time.

Lauer: It must Indeede Captaine, besides. doe ye not see, he has gotten a guard of ffrend*e*s about him as yf he had some knowledge of or purpose.

Du: had he a guard of Devills, as I thinke them litle better, my sword shold do the message that it came for.

Lauer yf you wilbee so desperat the blood lye vppon yor owne neck, for wee'le not medle int; [Fol. 16a]

Dubois Runs vpon Montagne, and struglinge yeilds him his Sword: the Officers drawe: Lauerdure, and Lapoope: retires: Montagne chaseth em About the stage: himselfe wounded:

1244 [1]*the*] interlined with a caret 1256 *on*] interlined with a caret 1263 *ffrendes*] [1]*f* written over erased *h*
1267] folio number ·(*16*· above and to the right of this line

Du: I am yor frend and servant,
struggle wth me, & take my sword. — } *they fight:*
noble sir. make yor waie, you haue slaine an officer,

Mont: some one of them has certainlye
requited me, for I doe loose much blood. – *Exit:*

·1· Offi: spretious, wee haue lost a brother, pursue the gent.

·2· Offi: Ile not medle wth him, you see what comes on't,
besides I knowe he wilbe hangd ere he be taken.

·1· Off: I tell thee yeoman, he must be taken ere he bee
hangd, he is hurte in the gutt*es*, run afore therefore,
& knowe how his wife will rate his sawsiges a pound.

·3· Off: staye brother, I may liue. for surelye I finde I am
not hurte in the leg. ——————— ~~[*Exit*]~~ *Exeunt*

Actus: 3: Scæna: 1: }

Ent: Maddam Lamira: Ladye Orleance: And Viramour the Page:

Lamira: you see ladye,
what harmlesse sport*es* o^{r} country life affoord*es*,
& though you meete not here wth cittye daintyes,
or courtlye Entertainement, what you haue.
is free, and hartye.

Lady: Orle: madame, I finde here
what is a stranger to the court, content,
& receaue courtesies donne for themselues,
wthout an expectation of returne,
wch byndes me to yor seruice.

Lamira: oh, yor loue.
my homely house, built more for vse then showe,
obserues the golden meane eaquily distant
from glittering pompe, & sordid *Auarice*.
for masques, wee will obserue the works of nature,
& in the place of visitation, read.
o^{r} phisick shalbee wholesome walkes, o^{r} viand*es* [Fol. 16b]
nourishing, not prouoakinge, for I finde
pleasures are tortures, that leaue stinge*s* behinde,

1296 *themselues*] *m* heavily inked

Lady: Orle: you haue a great estate

Lamy: a competencye
sufficient to maintaine me & my ranck,
nor am I, I thancke heaven, so courtlye bred
as to Imploye the vtmost of my Rent*es*
in payinge tailores for phantastick roabes,
or rather then be second in a ffashion,
eate out my officers & my revennewes
wth grating vsurie; my back shall not
be the base on wch yor soothing Cittizen
erect*es* his som̄er house, nor on the other side
will I be so pennuriouslye wise
as to make monye that*es* my slave, my Idole,
wch yet to wronge, meritt*es* as much reprofe,
as to abuse or servant.

Lady: Orl: yet, wth yor pardon.
I thinke you want the crowne of all contentment.

Lamy: In what good maddam.

Lady: Orl: In a worthy husband.

Lamy: humh, it is strange the gallye slaue shold praise
his ore, or stroakes, or you, that haue made shipwrack
of all delight vpon this rocke call'd marriage,
shold singe *Encomions* of't.

L: Orle: madame, though one fall
from his horse and breake his neck, will you
conclude from that it is vnfit to ride,
or must It follow because *Orleance*
my lord is pleasd to make his passionate triall
of my suspected patience. that my brother.
were he not so, (I might saie worthy *Amience*).
will Imitate his Ills, that cannot fancie
what*es* truly noble in him,

Lamy: I must grante
theres as much worth in him, as can be lookt for
from a yonge lord. but not ynough to make

1316 *vsurie*] *v* blotted 1318 *som̄er*] *m* blotted 1330 *Encomions*] *c* written over erased letter

me change my golden libertye. and consent
to be a servant to it, as wiues are
to the Imperious humors of their lord*e*s.
me thinkes I am well I rise. & goe to bed
when I thinke fit, eate what my appetite [Fol. 17a]
desires, wthout controwle. my servant*e*s studye
is my contentment, & to make me merrie
their farthest ayme. my sleepes are Enquirde after,
my rising vp saluted wth respect
com̄ande and libertye now waites vpon
my virgin state, what wolld I more, change all
& for a husband, no, these freedomes dye
in wch they liue; with my virginitie,
tis in hir choise that*e*s rich to be a wife,
but not being yoak't, to choose the single life.
boy.

Viramour: maddam

Lamy: how like you the country.

Vira: I like the ayre of it well madame. & the rather, because as In Irish timber yor spider will not make his web, so for ought I see that yor cheater. pander. & Informer being in there dispositions to ffoggie for this peircing clymate. shun it, & chuse rather to walke in mist*e*s. in the Cittie.

Lamy: who did you serue first boy.

Vira: a rich marchant*e*s widdow, & was by her preferd to a yonge court ladye.

Lady: Orle: and what difference found you in their seruice.

Vira: very much, for looke how much my olde cittye madame gaue to hir yonge visitant*e*s, so much my ladye receau'd from her hoarye court servant*e*s.

Lamy: and what made you to leaue hir.

Vira: my ffather (maddam) haueing [had] a desire to haue me a tall man, tooke me from thence,

1347] folio number (*17* above and to the right of this line 1355 *with*] *wi* altered, possibly from *in* 1361 *Vira:*] *i* altered from *e* 1375 *haueing*] interlined with a caret

Lamy: well. I perceaue you Inherit the wagg, from yor ffather.

Vira: *Doues* beget *Doues*: and *Eagles Eagles* madame, a
cittizens heire tho' left never so rich, seldome at
the best proues but a griffin gent; the son of an
Advocate, tho' dubd like his ffather, will showe a relish
of his decent & the ffathers thriuinge practize;
as I haue heard she that of a chambermaide is
metamorphosed into a madame, will yet remember
how oft her daughter by hir mother venterd to lye
vpon the rushes, before she coo'd get in that wch makes
manye ladyes.

L: Orle: but what thinke you of yor late mr. [Fol. 17b]

Vir: oh madame: —} *Sighes.*

Lamy: why doe you sighe. you are sorrie that you left him,
he made a wanton of you

Vira: not for that,
or yf he did: for that my youth must loue him.
oh pardon me, yf I saie libertye
is bondage, yf compared wth his kinde seruice.
& but to haue power now to speake his worth[.]
to ites desert, I shold be well content
to be an old man when his praise were Ended.
& yet yf at this Instant you were pleasd[.]
I shold begin, the liuery of age
wolld take his lodging vp vppon this heade
ere I shold bring it to a period..
in breife he is a man. (for heaven forbid
that ever I shold liue to saie hee was.
of such a shape as wolld make one beloued
that never had good thought. & to his bodye
he hath a minde of such a constant temper,
in wch all vertues thronge to haue a roome.
yet gainst this noble gent, this *Montagne*,
for in that name I comprehend all goodnes,
wronge, & the wrested law, falce wittnesses,

1381 *like*] interlined with a caret

& Envye sent from hell, haue rose in armes,
& tho' not peirc'd, batterd this honord sheild
what shall I saie. I hope you will forgiue me,
that but yor selfe. yf you were pleasd to loue,
Ent: Charlot: \ wth A letter / I knowe no *Iuno* worthye such a *Ioue*.

Lamy: tis well yet, that I haue the second place
in yor affection. – from whence.

Charlote: from the lord of *Amience* madame.

Lamy: tis wellcome, though it beare his vsuall language. –
I thought so much: his loue sute speaks his health,
[————]
'twolld showe well in a night cap.

L: Orle: but in him I hope as he meanes, appeares honorable.

Lamy: on those termes I receaue it. whates he that brought (it.

Charl: a gent of good ranck it seemes.

Lamy: where is hee.

Charl: receauing Entertainement In yor house,
sorting his degree.

Lamy: tis well

Charl: he waites yor ladiships pleasure. [Fol. 18a]

Lamy: he shall not waite longe.
Ile leaue you for a while. nay staye you boy.
attend the ladye. ——— *Exe: Lamyra. et Charlote.*

Vir: wolld I might liue once
to waite on my poore m^{r}.

L: Orle: thates a good boy.
this thankefulnes looks louely on thy forehead,
& in it as I booke me thinks I read
Instructions for my selfe that am his debtor.
& wolld do much that I might be so happie
to repaire that wch to o^{r} greife is ruind.

1418 *whence*] *w* written over erased *h* 1421] rule deleted after this line 1431] folio number *(18.* above and to the right of this line 1438 *forehead*] ^{2}*e* altered from *a* 1440 *debtor*] *o* altered from *e*

Vira: It were a worke a king might glorye in,
t: Montaigne= yf he sawe wth my eyes. yf you please madame
for sure to me you seeme vnapt to walke,
to sit, although the churlish birdes denye
to giue vs musique in this groue, where they
are prodigall to others, Ile straine my voice
for a sad *Songe*, the place is safe, & priuat.

L: Orle: twas my desire. begin good *Viramour*.

Songe:*] *At the Ende of it: Ent: Montagne: fainting his Sword drawne:

L: Orle: whates he *Viramour*.

Vira: a goodly personage.

Mont: am I yet safe, or is my flight a dreame
my woundes, and hunger tell me that I [walke] wake.
[wr] whither haue my feares borne me. no matter
who hath no place to goe to, cannot er, (where,
what shall I doe? cunning calamitye
that others grosse wittes vses to refine,
when I most neede it, dulls the edge of myne.

L: Orle: Is not this *Montagnes* voice.

Vir: my mr, fye.

Mont: what sounde was that, pish.
feare makes the wretch thinke every leafe a Iurye.
what course to liue, beg. better men haue done it,
but in another kinde. steale. *Alexander*.
though stiled a conqueror. was a prowde theefe,
though he robd wth an armye. fye how Idle
these meditations are. though thou art worse
then sorrowes tongue can speake thee, thou art still
or sholdst be, honest *Montagne*.

L: Orle: tis too true [Fol. 18b]

Vira: tis hee.
what villaines hande did this? oh that my flesh
weare balme. Infaith sir I wolld pluck it of
as readilye as this: pray you accept
my will to doe you seruice. I haue heard

the mouse once saued the lyon in his neede,
as the poore *Scarab* spild the *Eagles* seede.

L: Orle: how do you.

Mont: as a forsaken man.

L: Orle: doe not say so, take comfort,
for yor misfortunes haue beene kinde in this
to cast you on a hospitable shoare,
where dwells a ladye,

Vira: she to whome good m^{r}. you preferrd me.

L: Orle: In whose house. what so ere
yor dangers are. Ile vndertake yor safetye

Mont: I feare I am pursued, & doubt that I
in my defence haue killd an officer

Vira: Is that all. theres no law vnder the *Sun*
but will I hope confesse one drop of blood
shed from this arme, is recompence ynough
though you had cut the throtes of all the catchpoles
in *ffrance*, nay in the world

Mont: I wolld be loath
to be a burthen, or feed like a droane
on the Industrious labour of the *Bee*,
& baser far, I hold it, to owe for
the breade I eate, what*e*s not in me to pay
then that since my full fortunes are declined
to their low ebb. I fashion my high minde.
It was no shame to *Hecuba* to serue
when *Troy* was firde, yf't be in yor power
to be a meanes to make hir Entertaine me,
& far from that I was, but to supplye
my want wth habit fit for him that serues,
I shall owe much to you.

L: Orle: leaue that care to me.

Vira: good sir leane on my sholder,
helpe good madame. oh that I were a horse for halfe

1498 *feed*] ^{2}*e* interlined with a caret   1504 *was*] *as* altered

an houre that I might carry you home, on my back.
I hope you will loue me still,

Mont: thou doest deserue it boy.
that I sholld liue to be thus troblesome, [Fol. 19a]

L: Orle: good sir, tis none.

Vira: troble most willingly. I wolld be changd
like *Apuleius*; weare his asses eares.
prouided I might still this burthen beare.

L: Orle: tis a kinde boy

Mont: I finde true proofe of it. ———— *Exeunt*

Ent: Amience: Longauile: hauing A paper in's hand.

Amie: youle carrie it

Longa: as I liue I will, although my packet were like *Belerophons*
what haue you seene in me or my behauior since yor
fauors so plentifully showerd vpon my wantes, that may
beget distrust of my performance.

Amie: nay be not angrie yf I Entertaind
but the least scruple of yor loue, or courage
I wolld make [choice] purchase of one wth my state
shold doe me right in this, nor can you blame me
yf in a matter of such consequence
I am so Importunate.

Long: good my lord, let me prevent yor further coniurations,
to raise my spiritt. I knowe this is a chalenge
to be deliuerd vnto *Orleance* hand.
& that my vndertakeing Endes not there.
but I must be yor second, & in that
not a loone search yor Enimie. measure weapons,
but stande in all yor hazardes, as or bloodes
ran in the selfe same veines, in wch yf I
better not yor opinion; as a limbe

1514 *me*] *e* blotted 1516] folio number *(19* above and to the right of this line 1525 *Belerophons*] *s* interlined with a caret 1531 *purchase*] interlined with a caret

that*es* putrified & vselesse, cut me of,
and vnderneath the gallowes burye It.

Amie: At full you vnderstand me, & in this
bynde me & what*es* myne to you & yo^{res}.
I will not so much wronge you as to ad
one sillable more, let it suffice I leaue
my honor to yor guard. & in that [prooue] proue
you hold the first place in my harte, & loue. – <u>*Exit*</u>

Long: the first place in a lord*es* affection? very good, and how
long doth that last, perhaps the changing of some three
shirt*es* at tennis, well, yt were verie necessarye, that
an order were taken, (yf it were possible) that yonger
br⟨o⟩thers might haue more wit, or more monye, for now
how ever the foole hath long beene put vppon him that [Fol. 19b]
Inherit*es* [thee] his [best] revennew, hath brought him a spungee
& wipt of the Imputation, & for the vnderstanding of
the yonger, let him get as much rhetorick as he can
Ent: Dubois: — to grace his language, they will see he shall glosse
litle ynough to set out his barck. – stand *Dubois*.
looke about. all safe,

Dub: approch not neere me but wth reverence,
Laurell and adoration, I haue done more
[I haue done more] then deserues 10000 duckett*es*.

Long: how now, what*es* the matter.

Dub: wth this hand, only, ayded by this braine,
wthout an *orpheus* harpe, redeemd from hells
three headed porter o^{r} *Euridice*.

Long: nay prethee speake sence. this is like the stale bragart
in a playe

Dub: then in plaine proze thus, & wth as litle action as thou
canst desire, the three headed porter, was three
vnexorable catchpoles, out of whose Iawes. wthout the
helpe of *orpheus* harpe, bayle, or bribe, for those too

1558 *[thee]*] altered to *he* before being deleted *his*] interlined with a caret 1563 *looke*] *lo* altered 1569 *harpe*] *h* altered

stringes makes the musique that mollifies those flinty
furies, I rescued o^{r} *Euridice*: I meane my old m^{r} *Montagne*.

Long: & is this all, a poore rescue. [pretious tis allmost as cōmon
as to haue a lord arrested, & lye by' it.] I thought thou
had'st reuerst the Iudgment for his overthrow, in his
sute, or wrought vpon his adversarie *Orleance*, taken
the shape of a ghost, frighted his minde into distraction,
& for the appeasing of his conscience forc'd him to
make restitution of *Montagnes* lande*s*! or such like! rescued?
light I wolld haue hyred a *Croiheture* for 2· crownes
to haue done so much wth his whip.

Dub: you wold sir, & yet it is more then three one their ffoot=
clothes durst doe for a sworne brother in a coach

Long: besides, what proofe of It, for ought I knowe this may
be a trick. I had rather haue him in prison where I
might visit him & doe him seruice then not at all,
or I knowe not where.

Dub: well sir, the Ende will shewe it. whate*s* that a chalenge.

t: Orlean: *Long:* yes, wheres *Orleance*. though wee fight in Ieast, hee
must meete wth *Amience* in Earneste. — fall of. wee are discouerd,

Orle: my hou⟨se⟩. garsoon, ha!

Dub: weare it not in a house, & in his house [Fol. 20a]
to whome I owe all dutie.

Long: what wolld it doe, prate as it does, but be as far
from strikeing, as he that owes it, *Orleans*.

Dub: how?

Long: I thinke thou art his porter.
set heere to answer creditors, that his lordship
is not wthin, or takes the diet. I am sent
& will growe heere, vntell I haue an answer,
not to dem̄aund a debt of monye, but
to call him to a strict accompt for wronge
donne to the honor of a gent,
wch nothing but his heart*es* blood shall wash of.

1579 *this*] *t* altered 1588 *is*] *s* altered 1598] folio number (*20·* above and to the right of this line
1605 *takes*] *es* altered 1610 *wash*] *s* altered from another letter

Dub: shall I heare this:

Long: & more, that yf I maye not
haue accesse to him, I will fix this heere,
to his disgrace & thine.

Dub: & thy life wth it.

Long: then haue the coppies of it pasted on postes.
like pamphlet titles that sue to be sould,
haue his disgrace talke of tobacco shopps,
his picture baffeld.

Dub: all respect awaye, wert in a church, —} *drawe both*

Long: this is the booke I pray wth.

Orle: forbeare vpon yor liues.

Long: what? are you rowsd. I hope yor lordship can read, (though
you staine not yor birth wth scholership,) doth it not please
you, now yf you are a right *Monsir*, muster vp the
rest of yor attendance, wch is a page, a cooke, a pandar,
coachman, & a ffootman, in these dayes a great lord*e*s
traine; pretending I am vnworthy to bringe you a
chalenge Insteed of answering it, [haue] thrust me downe
the staires,

Dub: yf he does. thou deseru'st it.

Long: I dare you both to touch me, Ile not stand still.
what answere you.

Orle: that thou hast donne to *Amience*
the office of a faithfull frend, wch I
wolld cherish in thee were he not my foe.
however, since on honorable termes
he calls me forth, say I will meete wth him,
& by *Dubois* ere *Sun* set make him knowe
the time & place, my sword*e*s lenght, & what ever
scruple of circumstance, hee can expect. [Fol. 20b]

Long: this answer comes vnlookt for, fare you well.
findeing yor temper thus, wold I had saide lesse.
— *Exit*

1617 *pamphlet*] *h* altered, ? from *l* 1624 *it*] blotted

Orle: now comes thy loue to the test.

Dub: my lord 'twill hold,
& in all dangers proue it selfe true gold. — *Exeunt*

Enter: Lauerdure: Lapoope: Malycorne: & A Seruant:

Seruant: I will aquainte my ladye wth yor cominge,
please you repose yor selues heere.

Maly: theres a tester, nay now I am a wooer, I must be
bountifull.

Seru: yf you wolld haue too 3·pences for it sir,
t: Montaigne: to giue some of yor kindred as you ride, Ile see yf I can
mira: Lady Orleance \ get em wee vse not (tho' servant*e*s) to take bribes. – Exit.
arlot: Page: *but I may spare my labour heeres my lady*

Lauer: then thou art vnfit to bee in office either in court or cittye.

Lapoop: Indeed corruption is a tree, whose branches are of an
vnmeasurable lenght, they spread every where, & the dewe
that drops from them haue Infected some chaires and
stooles of authoritie.

Maly: oh Captaine lay not all the fault vppon officers. you
knowe you can sharke though you be out of action,
witnes *Montagne*.

ap] *Lauer:* hange him, hees safe ynough. you had a hand in it too, &
haue gained by him, but I wonder you cittizens, that keepe
so manye shop=books, & take such strickt accounte for every
farthing due to you from others, reserue not so much as
a memorandum for the curtesies you receaue,

Maly: wolld you haue a cittizen booke those; [thing*e*s] thankefulnes
is a thinge wee're not sworne too in or Indentures, you
may as well vrge conscience.

Lauer: talke no more of such vanities. *Montagne* is Irrecouerablye
sunck, I wold wee had 20· more to send after him,
the snake that wolld be a dragon & haue wing*e*s, must
eate a spider: & what Impl[o]yes that but this? that
in this *Canniball* age, he that wolld haue the sute of
wealth, must not care whome he feedes on. & as I haue

1656] interlined by Hand 2

heard, no flesh battons better, then that of a profest
frend, & hee that wold mount to honor, must not make
daintye to vse the head of his mother, back of his father,
or necke of his brother; for ladders to his preferment, for
but obserue, & you shall finde for the most parte cuning
villanye sit at a feaste, as principall guest, & Inocent [FOL. 21a]
honestie waite as a contemnd servant wth a trencher,

Ent: Montagne: bare: Lamyra: Lady Orleance: Charlot: Viram:

Lapo: the ladyes.

Mon: do ye smell nothing.

Charl: not I sir.

Mont: the carrion of three knaves is verye strong in my nosthrill.

Lauer: wee came to admire, & ffinde fame was a nigard
wch wee thought prodigall in yor report,
before wee sawe you.

Lamy: tush sir, this courtships olde.

Lapoop: Ile fight for thee sweet wench,
this is my tongue & wooes for me.

Lamy: good man of warr
handes of, yf you take me it must be by seige,
not by an onsett, & for yor vallor. I
thinke that I haue deserued few Enimyes,
& therefore neede it not.

Maly: thou needst nothing sweet lady but an obsequious
husband, & where wilt thou finde him yf not in the
cittye, wee are true *Muscouites* to o^{r} wiues, & are
never better pleasd then when they vse vs as slaues,
bridle & sadle vs, haue me thou shalt cōmaund all,
my wealth is thine owne, thou shalt sit like a *Queene* in
my warehouse, & my ffactors at their returne wth my
shipps, shall pay thee tribute of all the rarietyes
of the Earth. thou shalt weare gold, feede on delicates,
the first peascodes, strawberyes, grapes, cherries, shall

1684] folio number (*21* above and to the right of this line 1687 *the*] *t* blotted 1692 *ffinde*] ^{1}*f* written over erasure

Lamy: be myne, I apprehend what you wolld saie,
those daintyes wch the Cittye payes so deare for.
the Country yeild*e*s for nothing, & as early.
& credit me yon far fecht viand*e*s please not
my appetite better then those that are neere hand.
then for yor promise seruice. & subiection,
to all my humors, when I am yor wife,
(wch as It seemes is frequent in the cittye),
I cannot finde what pleasure they receaue
in vseing theire fond husband*e*s like their maid*e*s,
but of this more hereafter, I accept
yor proffer kindlye, & yo^{res}, my house stand*e*s open
to Entertaine you take yor pleasure in it,
& ease, after yor Iornye,

L: Orle: doe you note the boldnes of these fellowes

Lamy: Alas madame, a virgin must in this be like a lawier. [FOL. 21b]
& as hee taks all ffees, so she must here all suitors,
the one for gaine, the other for hir mirth. staye wth
the gent, wee'le to the orchard. — *Exe: Vir: & woemen,*

Lapoop: hum, what art thou,

Mont: an honest man though poore,
& looke [they] such like to monsters, are they so rare.

Lauer: rise from the dead.

Maly: doe you heare, *Monsir* seruiture, didst thou never heere
of one *Montagne*, a prodigall gull that liues about
Paris.

Mont: so sir.

Lauer: one that after the losse of his maine estate in a law
sute, bought an office in the court.

Lapoop: and shold haue had letters of *Mart*, to haue taken
the spanish treasure as It came from the *Indyes*,
weare not thou & hee twins, put of thy hat let me
see thy forhead.

myra showes Selfe at the Arras:

1734 *such*] interlined with a caret

Mont: though you take priuiledge to vse yor tongues,
I pray you hold yor ffingers,
'twas yor base coosnage made me as I am,
& were you some where else, I wolld take of
the prowde filme [of] from yor eyes, that will not let
you knowe I am *Montagne*

Lamy: I will obserue this better

Lapoop: & art thou hee? I will do thee grace, giue me thy hand,
I am glad thou hast taken so good a course, serue god
& please thy m^{r}s; yf I proue to be thy m^{r}, as I am
verie likely, I will doe for thee.

Maly: faith, the fellowes well made for a servingman, and
will no doubt carry a chine of beefe wth a good
grace.

Lapoop: prethee be carefull of me in my chamber, I will
remember thee at my departure,

Mont: All this I can Indure vnder this roofe,
& so much owe I her, whose now, I am,
that no wronge shall Incense me to molest
hir quiet house, while you continew heere
I will not be ashamd to doe you seruice,
more then to hir, because such is hir pleasure,
but you that haue broke thrice, & fourtene tymes
compounded for 2·^{s} in the pounde,
knowe I dare kick you, in yor shop do you heare
yf ever I see *Parris*: though an armye
of mustye murrions, Rusty browne bills, & clubbs [FOL. 22a]
stand for yor guard. I haue heard of yor trick*e*s.
& you that smell of amber, at my charge,
& triumphe in yor cheate, well. I may liue
to meete thee, bee it amonge a troope of such
that are vpon the faire face of the courte
like ronninge vlcers, & before thy whore
trample vpon thee,

Lapoop: Is this a language for a liuorye? take heede, I am a
(Captaine.

1760 *of*] *o* written over *,*   1772] folio number *(22.* above and to the right of this line

Mont: a Coxcombe are you not? that thou & I
to giue proofe wch of vs dares most, weare now
in midst of a rough sea, vpon a peece
of a split ship where onlye one [my] might ride,
I wolld – but foolish anger makes me talke I knowe not
(what,

Ent: Lamyra:
om the Aras

Indeed you act a parte
doth Ill become my servant. is this yor dutye.

Mont: I craue yor pardon, & will hereafter be more circumspect,

Lauer: oh the power of a woemans tongue. It hath done more
then wee three wth or sword*es* durst vndertake, put a
madman to silence.

Lamy: why sirra, these are none of yor comrades,
to drinke wth in the celler, one of them
for ought you knowe, maye liue to be yor mr.

Lapoop: theres some comfort yet,

Lamy: heeres choice of three, a wealthye marchant,

Maly: hem. shees taken. she hath spyed my good calfe,
& manye ladyes chuse their husband*es* by that.

Lamy: a Courtier that*es* in grace, a valiant captaine,
& are these mates for you, awaie, be gone,

Mont: I humbly praie you will be pleasd to pardon
& to giue satisfaction to you madame,
(although I breake my harte,) I will confesse
that I haue wrongd them, too, & make submission.

Lamy: no, Ile spare that, goe, bid the Cooke haste supper.

–Exit Mont

Lapoop: did she talke of supper. oh braue ladye, thou art
worthy to haue servant*es*, to be cōmandresse of a familye,
that knowest how to vse & gouerne it,

Lauer: you shall haue manye mrses, that will so mistake, as to
take their horsekeepers, & ffootemen insteed of theire
husband*es*, thou art none of those,

1785 *might*] interlined with a caret   1796 *for … mr.*] followed by '___ here' in pencil

Maly: [but she] *I loue a lady* that can make a distinction of men, & knowes
when she hath gallant*e*s, & fellowes of ranck & quallitie
in hir house,

Lamy: gallant*e*s Indeed, yf it be the gallant*e*s ffashion [FOL. 22b]
to triumph In the miseries of a man.
of wch they are the cause, one that transcend*e*s
(in spight of all that ffortune hath or can)
a million of such thing*e*s as you, my doores
stand open to receaue all such as weare
the shape of gent̃, & my gentlier nature
(I might saie weaker) wayes not the expence
of Entertainement, thinke you Ile forget, yet
what*e*s due vnto my selfe, doe not I knowe
that you haue dealt wth poore *Montagne*, but like
needy cōmanders, cheating cittizens,
& periurd Courtiers. I am much mou'd,
Else vse not to saie so much. yf you will
beare yor selues as fitt*e*s such you wolld make me
thinke you are you maye staie, the waie lyes before
(you. – *Exit*

Maly: what thinke you of this Captaine,

Lapoop: that this is a bawdye house, wth pinacles & turrett*e*s,
in wch this disguised *Montagne* goes to rut gratis, &
that this is a landed pandresse, & maks hir house
a brothell for charitye;

Maly: come, that*e*s no wonder. but from whence deriue you this[.]
supposition.

Lauer: obserue but the circumstance, you all knowe that in the
height of *Montagnes* prosperitie, he did affect & had
his loue returnd by this lady *Orleance*, since her diuorce
=ment & his decaye of estate, it is knowne they haue
met, not; so much as his boy is wanting, & that this
can be anye thinge else then a meere plott for there
night worke is aboue my Imagination to conceave,

1815 *I . . . lady*] interlined by Hand 2 1840 *but*] interlined with a caret

Maly: nay It carries probabillitie, let vs obserue it better,
but yet wth such caution as or prying be not discouerd.
heeres all thinges to be had wthout cost, & therefore
nt: Viramoor: – good staying heere.

Lapoop: nay thates true, I wolld wee might woo [wooe] her 20· yeares
:nt: Viramoor]: –like *Penelopes* suitors, come *Lauerdure*. – *Ext: Maly et Lapoop*

Lauer: I follow Instantlye, yonder hee is, the thought of this
boy. hath much cool'd my affection to his ladye,
& by all coniectures, this is a disguisd whore, I
will try If I can search this mine, *Page*, [FOL. 23a]

Vir: yor pleasure sir,

Lauer: thou art a pretty boy.

Vir: and you a braue man, now I am out of yor debt.

Lauer: nay prethee staye.

Vir: I am in haste sir,

Lauer: by the faith of a courtier

Vir: take heede what you saie, you haue taken a strange oath,

Lauer: I haue not seene a youth that hath pleased me
better, I wolld thou couldst like me so far as to leaue
thy ladye & waite on me, I wolld maintaine thee in the
brauest clothes.

Vir: though you tooke them vp one trust, or bought them at
the brokers.

Lauer: or any waie, then thy Emploimentes shold be so neate &
cleanly thou sholdst not touch a paire of pantables
in a month, & thy lodging

Vir: shold be in a brothell

Lauer: no, but in myne armes

Vir: that may be the circle of a baudye house, or worse,

Lauer: I meane thou sholdst lye wth me,

1853 *Lapoop:*] interlined *woo*] altered, possibly from *woe* [*wooe*]] interlined 1859] folio number (*23*. above and to the right of this line

Vir: lye wth you. I had rather lye wth my ladyes monkey.
twas never a good world since o^{r} [ffrench lord*es*] gallant*es* learned
of the *Neapolitans* to make theire pages their bedfellows,
it dothe more hurt to the suburbe ladyes, then twenty
dead vacations, tis supper time sir, — *Exit Vir.*

Lauer: I thought so. I knowe by that tis a woeman, because
peradventure she hath made tryall of the monckye
she prefers him before me as one vnknowne. well,
these woemen are strange creatures, & haue strange desires,
& men must vse strange meanes to quench strange fires,
Exit

Actus Quartij: Scæna: Prj

Enter Montaigne: in meane habit:

Mont: now *Montaigne*, who discernes thy spirit now,
thy breeding, or thy blood, heeres a poore clowd
eclipseth all thy splendor, who can reade
in thy pale face. dead eye, or lenten sute
the libertye thy ever giuing hand
hath bought for others, manacling it selfe
In gyves of parchment Indisoluable, [FOL. 23b]
the greatest harted man supplyed wth meanes,
nobilitye of birth, & gentlest part*es*,
I, though the right hand of his soueraigne,
yf vertue quit hir seate in his high soule,
glitters but like a pallace set on fire,
whose glorye whilst it shines but ruins him
& his bright showe each houre to ashes tending
shall at the last be raekt vp like a sparkle,
vnlesse mens lives and fortunes feede the flame,
not for myne owne want*es* though, blame I my starrs,
but suffering others to cast loue on me,
when I can neither take, nor thankefull bee,
my ladyes woman, faire & vertuous,
yonge as the present month, solicit*es* me
Ent: Viramour: for loue, & marriage, now being nothing worth

1881 *gallantes*] interlined 1899 *Indisoluable*] *I* altered 1904 *glitters*] *e* blotted 1908] followed by a blank line

Vir: oh m^{r}, I haue sought you a long houre.
good faith I never Ioye out of yor sight.
for heavens sake sir be merrie, or else beare
the buffet*e*s of yor ffortune wth more scorne,
doe but begin to raile. teach me the waye,
& Ile sit downe & helpe yor anger forth,
I haue knowne you weare a sute full worth a
giuen to a man whose neede nere frighted you (lordship
from calling of him frend, fiue hunderd crownes,
ere sleepe had left yor sences to consider
yor owne Important present vses, yet
since I haue seene you wth a trencher waite,
voide of all scorne, therefore Ile waite on you,

Mont: wolld heaven thou weart lesse honest.

Vir: wolld to heaven you were lesse worthy,
I am even with you sir.

Mont: Is not thy m^{r} strangely fallne. when thou
seruest for no wages, but for charitie;
thou doest surcharge me wth thy plentious loue,
the goodnes of thy vertue showne to me
more opens still my disabillitye
to quit thy paines, credit me louing boy
a free & honest nature may be opprest.
tired wth curtesies from a liberall spiritt
when they exceede his meanes of gratitude.

Vir: but tis a vice in him that to that end
extendes his loue or dutie

Mont: litle world
of vertue, why dost loue. & follow me,

Vir: I will follow you through all countryes. [Fol. 24a]
Ile ronne (fast as I can) by yor horse side,
Ile hold yor stirrop when you doe alight
& without grudging waite tell you returne,
Ile quit assurd meanes. & expose my selfe
to cold & hunger still to bee wth you,

1915 *a*] interlined with a caret
1944] folio number *(24.* above and to the right of this line; *2* altered, possibly from *1*
1945 *yor*] *o* blotted

fearelesse Ile travell through a wildernesse,
& when you are wearye, I will laye me downe,
that in my bosome you may rest yor head,
where whilst you sleepe, Ile watch that no wilde
(beast
shall hurte or trouble you, & thus weele brede a storye,
to make every hearer weepe
when they discourse o^{r} fortunes & o^{r} loues,

Mont: oh what a scoffe might men of woemen make,
yf they did knowe this boye. but my desire
is that thou wolldest not (as thou vsest still
when like a servant I mong servant*es* sit
waite on my trencher, fill my cups wth wine.
why sholdest thou doe this boy, prithee consider
I am not what I was.

Vir: curst be the day
when I forget that *Montaigne* was my lord
or not remember him my m^{r} still,

Mont: rather curse me wth whome thy youth hath spent
so manye houres, & yet vntaught to liue
by anye worldlie quallitie,

Vir: Indede you never taught me how to handle cardes
to cheate & cozen men with oathes & lyes,
those are the worldlye quallities to liue
some of o^{r} scarlet gallant*es* teach their boyes,
since stumbling fortune then leaves vertue thus,
let me leaue ffortune ere be vicious,

Mont: oh lad. thy loue will kill me.

Vir: by my troth I thinke In conscience I shall dye for you,
good m^{r} weepe not, doe you want ought S^{r},
will you haue anye monye, heres some siluer,
& heres a litle gould. 'twill serve to playe,
& put more troublesome thought*es* out of yor minde,
I pray sir take it, Ile get more wth singing,
& then Ile bring it you, my ladye gaue't me,

1955 *hurte*] *t* altered from *l*   1980 *siluer*] *i* altered

& by my troth it was not couetousnes,
but I forgot to tell you sooner on't,

Mont: alas boy. thou art not bounde to tell it me,
& lesse to giue it, by thee scarfes, & garters,
& when I haue monye I will giue thee a sword,
nature made thee a beauteous caskanet,
nt: Charlot: — to locke vp all the goodnesse of the earth,

Vir: O m^{r}. heres a gentlewoman, good sir steale awaye, [FOL. 24b]
you were wont to be a curious avoider of woemens
companie.

Mont: why boy, thou darest trust me any where, dar'st thou
(not.

Vir: I had rather trust you by a roreing lyon,
then a ravening woeman

Mont: why boy.

Vir: why truely she devoures more mans flesh.

Mont: I but she roares not boy.

Vir: no sir, why she is never silent, but when hir mouthes full,

Char: *Monsir Montaigne.*

Mont: my sweet fellow, since you please to call me so.

Vir: on my conscience she wolld be pleasd well ynough to,
call you bedfellow, oh m^{r}. doe not hold hir by the hand so.
a woeman is a lymebush, that catcheth all she toucheth.

Char: I do most dangerouslye suspect this boy to be a wench,
art thou not one, come hether, let me feele thee.

Vir: wth all my harte,

Char: why doste thou pull of thy gloue.

Vir: why to feele whether you be a boy or no.

Char: fy boy. goe too, Ile not looke yor head, nor combe yor locke
any more, yf you talke thus,

Vir: why Ile sing to you no more then,

Char: fy vppon't, how sad you are, a yonge gent̄, that was
the verie *Sun* of ffrance.

2006 *so*] written over .

Mont: but I am in the Eclipse now,

Char: suffer himselfe to be over ronne wth a lethargie
of melancholye, & discontent,
rowze vp thy spirit man. & shake it of.
a noble soule is like a ship at sea,
that sleepes at anchor when the *Oceans* calme,
but when she rages, & the winde blowes highe,
he cutt*es* his waie wth pride, & maiestie,
I wolld turne foole, or poet, or anye thing,
or marrye, to make you merrie, prethee let*es*
walke. good *Viramour* leaue thy mr, & me,
I haue verie Earnest businesse wth him,

Vir: pray doe you leaue my mr & me, wee were verie merie,
before you came, he does not couet woemens companies,
what haue you to doe wth him, come sir, will you goe,
yfaith his minde is stronger then to credit womens vowes,
& to puer to be capable of their loues,

Char: the boy is Iealous. sweet lad leave vs, my ladye calld
for you I sweare, that*es* a good child, theres a peece of
gold for thee, goe by thee a feather.

Vir: theres two peeces for you, doe you goe & by one, or what [Fol. 25a]
you will, or nothing so you goe, – nay then I see you wolld
haue me goe sir, why faith I will, now I perceaue
you loue hir better then you doe me, but heaven blesse
you what ever you doe or Intend, I knowe you are
a verie honest man, —— *Exit*

Char: still shall I wooe thee, whilst thy yeares reply.
I cannot, or I will not marrye thee.
why hast thou drawne the blood out of my cheeks
& giuen a quicker motion to my hart,
oh thou hast bred a feaver in my veines
calld loue, wch no phisitian can cure,
haue mercie on a maide whose simple youth

2030 *were*] *w* altered from *v* 2033 *minde*] *i* altered 2037 *goe*] *oe* partly washed out 2038] folio number *(25.* above and to the right of this line 2042 *Intend*] *I* altered from *E*

Mont: how yor example fairest teacheth me
a cerimonious Idolatrye.
by all the Ioye of loue, I loue thee better } *kneeles*
then I or any man can tell another,
& will expresse the mercie wch thou crau'st,
I will forbeare to marrie thee, consider
thou art natures heire in feature, & thy parent*e*s
faire Inheritance, rise wth these thought*e*s.
& looke [wth] on me but wth a womans eye,
a decay'd fellow, voide of meanes & spirit,

Char: of spirit.

Mont: yes, could I else tamely liue,
forget my ffathers bloud, waite, & make legg*e*s.
staine my best breeches. wth the servile dropps,
that falls from others draught*e*s.

Char: this vizard where with thou wolldst hide thy spirit,
is perspectiue. to showe it plainelier,
this vndervalew of thy selfe, is but
because I shold not by thee, what more speakes
greatnesse of man then valiant patience,
that shrinks not vnder his *fates* strongest strokes.
these *Romane* deathes, as falling on a sword,
openinge of veines, wth poison quenching thirst,
(wch wee erroniouslye doe stile the deedes
of the heroique & magnanimous man)
was dead-eyd cowardize, & white cheeke feare,
who doubting tiranye, & faintinge vnder
fortunes falce lotterye, desperatelye ran
to death for dread of death, that soules most stoute,
that bearing all mischance, dares last it out,
will you performe yor word & marrie me, [FOL. 25b]
t: Longauile: – when I shall call you too't

Mont: by faith I will,

Char: whose this alight*e*s here.

Long: wth leaue faire creature,
are you the ladye m^{res} of the house

2054 *another*] *a* blotted 2059 *on*] interlined with a caret 2071 *not*] interlined with a caret

Char: hir servant sir,

Long: I pray then fauor me to Informe yor ladye
& *Duke Orleance* wife, a busines of Importe
awaites em heere; & craues for speedye answer,

Char: are you in poste sir, —— *Exit*

Long: no, I am in sattin ladye. I wolld you wolld be in poste.

Char: *I will returne sweet instantly*
honest frend, do you belong to the house, I pray be couerd.

Mont: yes sir. I doe.

Long: ha! dreamest thou *Longauile*, sure tis not hee, sir, I shold
knowe you.

Mont: so shold I you, but that I am asham'd,
but though thou knowest me, prethee *Longauile*,
mocke not my pouertie, pray remember yor selfe,
showes it not strangelye for thy clothes to stand
wthout a hat to myne, mock me no more

Long: the pox Embroder me all over sir
yf ever I began to mock you yet
the devill on me why shold I weare velvet.
& silver lace, hart I will teare it of;

Mont: why madman,

Long: put on my hat, yes, when I am hangd I will
I could breake my head
for holding eyes that knew not you at first,
but time & fortune ronne yor courses wth him,
heele laugh & scorne you, when you showe most
(hate.

**Enter: Lamira: Ladye Orleance: Lauerdure:
Lapoop: Malycorne: Charlot: Viramour:**

Lamira: yor affaire *Monsir*

Long: doe you mocke me ladye

2092 *sattin*] *a* written over another letter, possibly *e* 2093 *Char: ... instantly*] written vertically by Hand 2 in the left margin and preceded by an *X*, with the place of insertion marked by an *X* beneath and before *no* in TLN 2092 2098 ^{1}*I*] written over erased letter

Lamira: yor busines Sr I meane

Ladye: regard yor selfe good *Monsir Longauile*,

Lamira: you are to negligent of yor selfe & place,
couer yor head sweet *Monsir*.

Long: mistake me not faire ladyes, by my blood.
tis not to you, nor you that I stand bare

Lauerd: nay sweet deere *Monsir*, let not be to vs then

Lapoop: a pox a complement, [FOL. 26a]

Maly: and a plague of manners,
pray hide yor head, you gallant*e*s vse to doo't

Long: and you yor forhead*e*s, why you needfull accessary rascalls,
that cannot liue wthout yor mutuall knaveries
more then a bawde, a pander or a whore,
from one another, how dare you suspect
that I stand bare to you, what make you heere,
shift yor house ladye of em, for I knowe em,
they come to steale yor napkins, & yor spoones,
looke to yor silver bodkin (gentlewoeman),
tis a dead vtensill, & page ware yor pocket*e*s.
my reverence is vnto this man my mr.
whome you wth protestations, & oathes
as highe as heaven, as deepe as hell, wch wolld
deceiue the wisest man of honest nature
haue cosend & abusd, but I may meete you,
& beate you one wth to'ther

Mont: peace, no more,

Long: not a word sir

Lauer: I am something thicke of hearing, what said hee.

Lapoo: I heare him, but reguard him not,

Maly: nor I. I am [ne] never angrye fasting,

Long: my loue keepes back my dutie, noblest ladye,
if husband or brother merit loue in you
prevent their daingers, this houre bring*e*s to triall

2125] folio number (*26* above and to the right of this line   2137 *vnto*] *v* altered from *t*

their heere-to sleeping hates, by this time each
wthin a yarde is of the others harte,
& met to proue their causes & their spirit*e*s
wch their Impartiall sword*e*s pointes. haste & saue,
or never meete them more, but at the graue. *Exit*

Ladye: oh my distracted harte, that my wrackt honor,
shold for a brothers, or a husband*e*s life, throwe the vndoing
(dice.

Lamira: *Amience* Engadged, yf he miscarye all my hopes & Ioyes
I now confesse it lowdlye are vndone,
caroch, & haste, one mynute may betraie
a life more worth then all time can repay — *Exe: Ladyes & Mont.*

Maly: hum, *Monsir Lauerdure*, pursues this boy extreamely, captaine
what will you doe.

Lapoop: anye thing but follow this land seruice, I am a sea captaine
you knowe, & to offer to part em, wthout wee could doo't like
watermen wth long staues, a quarter of a mile of might be
dangerous.

Maly: why then let*e*s retire & pray for em, I am resolud to staie the
event, abusd more then wee haue beene wee cannot be, wthout
they fall to flat beateing on's. & that were vnkindlye done [FOL. 26b]
yfaith. — *Exe: Maly. & Lapoop.*

Vir: never stirre but you are the troublesom'st asse that ere
I met wth. retyre, you smell like a woemans chamber,
she newly vp, before she haue pincht hir vapors in wth
hir cloathes.

Lauer: I will haunt thee like thy granams ghost, thou shalt
never rest for me,

Vir: well, a pox of yor muske tongue for me, I perceaue tis
vaine to conceale a secret, from you. beleeue it sir, Indeed
I am a woeman.

Lauer: why la: I knew't. this propheticall tongue of mine, never
faild me, my mother was halfe a witch. never anye
thing that she forespake but came to passe, a woeman,

2159 *Engadged*] [1]*d* interlined with a caret

how happie am I, now wee may lawfullye come togeather
wthout feare of hanging, sweet wench be gracious, In
honorable sorte I wooe, no otherwise.

Vir: faith. the truth is I haue lou'd you longe

Lauer: see. see

Vir: but durst not open it

Lauer: by gad I thinke so.

Vir: but breifely. when you bring it to the test, yf there be
not one gent in this house, will chalenge more Interest
in me, then you can, I am at yor disposure. — [*Exit*]

Lauer: oh *fortunatus*. I envie thee not
for cap or powch. this day Ile proue my fortune
in wch yor lady doth elect her husband,
who wilbe *Amience*. 'twill saue my wedding dinner,
pouera Lapoop, & *Malycorne*, yf all faile
I will turne cittizen, a beautious wife
is the hornebooke to the richest tradesmans life. *Exeunt*

t: Dubois: Orleance: Longauile: Amience:
·2· Lacqueyes: A Page wth ·2· Pistolls:

Dubois: heeres a good even peece of ground my lord.
will you fixe heere,

Orle: yes, any where. *Lacquey*, take of my spurrs.
vppon a bridge, a rayle, but my swordes bredth,
vppon a battlement I'de fight this quarrell

Dubois: a' the ropes my lord.

Orle: vpon a line

Dubo: so all or country *Duells*, are carried like a fire worke, on

Orle: goe now staie wth the horses, & do you heare, (a thred.
vpon yor liues tell some of vs come to you,
dare not to looke this waie

Dub: Except you see strangers, or others, that by chance [Fol. 27a]
or purpose are like to Interrupt vs,

2192 *gad*] *a* written over ? *o* 2216] folio number (27. above and to the right of this line

Orle: then giue warning.

Long: who takes a sword. th'advantage is so small,
as he that doubt*e*s, hath the free leave to choose.

Orle: come, giue me any, & search me. tis not ground,
weapon, or second*e*s, that can make odd*e*s
in these fatall trialls, but the cause.

Amie: most true, & but it is no tyme to wish
when men are come to doe, I wolld desire
the cause 'twixt vs. were other then it is,
but where the right is, there preuaile o^{r} sword*e*s
& if my sister haue out liu'd hir honor,
I doe not praye I may outliue hir shame.

Orle: yor sister *Amience* is a whore, at once.

Amie: you oft haue spoke that sence to me before,
but never in this language[,] *Orleance*,
& when you spoke it faire, & first, I told you
that it was possible, you might be abusd.
but now. since you forget yor manners, you shall free me
if I transgresse my custome, you doe lye
& are a villaine, wch I had rather yet
my sword had proued, then I beene forc'd to speake
nay giue vs leaue, & since you stand so [highly] haughtily
& highly on yor cause, let you & I
wthout Engageing these too gent, singly determine it,

Long: my lord, youle pardon vs

Dubo: I trust yor lordships meane not to doe vs that afront,

Amie: as how.

Dubo: wee kisse yor lordshipps hand, & come to serue you wth o^{r} sword*e*s.

Long: my lord, wee vnderstand o^{r} selues.

Dubo: wee haue had the honor to be calld
into the businesse, & wee must not now quit it on termes.

Amie: not termes of reason.

2233 *spoke*] *o* altered from *e* 2238 *beene*] *b* altered 2241 *too*] *oo* blotted

Long: no, no reason for the quiting of or calling,
Dubo: true, yf I be calld too't, I must aske no reason.
Long: nor heere none neither, wch is lesse, nor looke for't,
It is a fauor yf my throte be cut,
thin: cry: oh yor lordship does me, wch I never can
ay their Swords:– nor must haue hope how to requite – what noise.
ay their Swords: what crye is that. my lord vpon yor guard.
some trechery is a foote.

nt: Ladye Orleance: Lamira: Montaigne: 2· Lacqueys: Pag

Ladye: O, here they are.
my lord (deare ladye helpe me, helpe me all,
I haue so woefull Interest in both
I knowe not wch to feare for most, & yet [Fol. 27b]
I must prefer my lord, deere brother,
you are to vnderstanding & to noble,
to be offended when I knowe my dutye.
though scarce my teares will let me se to doe it.
Orle: out loathed strumpit
Lady: O my dearest lord.
yf wordes could on me cast the name of whore
I then were worthy to be both: but knowe
yor vnkindenesse cannot make me wicked,
& therefore sholld lesse vse that power vpon me.
Orle: was this yor art to haue these actors come,
to make the Enterlude. wthdraw could man
& if thy spirit be not frozen vp.
giue me one strooke yet at thee for my vengeance
Amie: thou shalt haue strokes & strokes, thou glorious voice,
tell thou bee'st thinner ayer then that thou talkest,
Lamy: my lordes. *Count Amience.*
Lady: princlye husband.
Orle: whore.

2270 *but*] *b* blotted

Lamy: you wrong hir Impudent lord, O that I had the bulke
of those dull men, looke how they stand, & no man
will revenge an Inocent ladye

Amie: you hinder it madame.

Lamy: I wolld hinder you. is there none else to kill him,

Lady: kill him madame. haue you learnd that bad language,
O repent, or by the motiue. they will both kill me,

Orle: then dye my Infamye.

Mont: hold bloodye man.

Orle: art thou there *Basiliske*.

Mont: to strike thee dead. but that thy *fate* deserues some waightier
(hand,

Dub: [swe]et my lord.

Orle: O, heeres a plot, you bring yor champion wth you,
madame *Adultresse*[.] yor *Adulterer*. [wth] out howling bitch wolfe.

Dub: good my lord

Orle: are you hir graces countenance, lady the receaver
to the poore vertuous cvppell.

Dub: sweet my lord.

Orle: sweet rascall, didst thou not tell me falce fellow,
this *Montaigne* heere was murderd.

Dub: I did so, but hee was falcer. & a worthlesse lord
like thy fowle selfe that would haue had it so.

Long: *Orleance*, tis true, & shall be proued vpon thee.

Mont: thy malice *Duke*, & this thy wicked nature
are all as visible as thou, but I borne to contemne
thy Iniuries, doe knowe, that though thy greatnesse
may corrupt a Iurye, & make a Iudge afeard, [FOL. 28a]
& carrye out a world of Euills wth thy title,
yet thou art not quit at home, thou bearest about thee
that, that doth charge thee, & condemne thee too.
the thing that greiues me more, & doth indeed

2296 *out*] interlined 2298 *are*] written over erased *&* 2309] folio number *(28* above and to the right of this line

displease me, is, to thinke that so much basenes
stand*es* heere to haue Encounterd so much honor,
pardon me my lord, what late my passion spoke,
when you prouoked my Innocence

Orle: yes. doe,
O flattery, courser then the sute he weares,
giue him a new one *Amience*

Amie: Orleance, tis heere nor tyme nor place, to Iest or raile
poorely wth you, but I will finde a time to
whisper you fourth to this, or some fit place,
as shall not hold a second Interruption.

Mont: I hope yor lordships honor & yor life
are destin'd vnto higher hazard*es*. this is of
to meane an arme

Dubo: yes faith, or none.

Long: he is not fit to fall by an honest sword,
a prince & lye,

Dubo: & slander. & hire men
to publish the falce rumors he hath made,

Long: and sticke em on his frend*es*, & Inocent*es*.

Dubo: and practise gainst their lives after their fames.

Long: In men that are the matter of all lewdnesse,
bawdes. theeues. & cheaters, it were monstrous.

Dubo: but in a man of blood. how more conspicuous.

Amie: can this be heaven.

Lady: they doe slander him

Orle: hang em. a paire of railing hang byes.

Long: how. stand *Orleance*. stay, giue me my pistolls boy,
hinder me not, by that foule life of wch
thou art no longer mr, I will kill thee.

Lady: O stay his ffurie,

Amie: *Longauile*, my frend

Long: not for my selfe my lord, but for mankinde
& all that haue an Interest to vertue,
or title vnto Innocence.

Amie: why here me.

Long: for Iustice sake

Amie: that cannot bee

Long: to punish his wiues. yor honors. & my lord*e*s wrong*e*s heere,
whome I must ever call so, for yor loues, I sweare Ile sacrific(

Amie: *Longauile*, I did not thinke you a murtherer before [FOL. 28b]

Long: I care not what you thought me.

Amie: by my [soule] [blood], & what it hopes for, yf thou attempt
his life, thy owne is forfet

Mont: ffoolish frantick man. the murder will be of vs, not him,

Lady: O heaven.

Mont: wee could haue killd him, but wee wolld not take
the Iustice out of *fates*. – before my god
sindge but a haire of him. thou dyest,

Long: no matter: —} *shootes:*

Amie: villaine.

Dubo: my lord, yor sister is slaine,

Lamy: *Biancha*:

Mont: O haplesse, & most wretched chance

Lamy: standst thou looking vpon the mischeefe thou hast made[,]
thou godlesse man, feeding thy blood shot eyes
wth the red spectacle, & art not turnd to stone,
wth horror, hence & take the wing*e*s, of thy black
Infamye to carrie thee beyond the shoote of lookes,
or sound of curses, wch will pursue thee tell
thou hast out fled all but thy guilte.
that still be present wth thee.

Orle: O wish it of againe; for I am crackd
vnder the burden. & my harte will breake,

2354 *murtherer*] 3*r* altered 2356 *[blood]*] interlined with a caret

how heavie guilt is, when men comes to feele.
[the burden of his] yf you could knowe the mountaine I sustaine
of horror, you wolld each take of yor parte,
& more to ease me. I cannot stand
forgiue where I haue wrongd I praye.

Amie: looke to him *Montaigne*

Long: my lord*e*s, & gent, the ladyes well but for hir feare,
vnlesse that haue shot her.
I haue the worst on't, that needes wolld venter
vpon a tricke, had like to haue cost my gut*e*s.
looke to hir, sheele be well, it was but powder
I charged wth, thinkeing that a guiltye man
wolld haue beene frighted sooner, but I am glad
hees come at last.

Lamy: how, is *Biancha* well

Mont: not hurt.

Amie: liues shee. see, sister, doth she breath.

Ladye: thinke you I can bre[.]ath
that am restored to the hatefull sence
of feeling in me my deere husband*e*s death
O no, I live not, life was that I left,
& what you haue calld me to is death Indeed
I cannot weepe so fast as hee doth bleed. [FOL. 29a]

Dubo: pardon me madame, hee is well

Lady: ha? my husband,

Orle: I cannot speake whether my Ioye or shame
be greater, but I thanke thee heaven for both
O looke not black vpon me all my frendes,
to whome I will be reconsiled, or growe vnto
this earth, tell I haue wept a trench
that shall be great Enough to be my graue,
& I will thinke them to most manly teares,
yf they doe moue yor pittyes. It is true,
man shold do[oe] nothing that he shold repent,

2384 *hir*] interlined with a caret 2395 *bre[.]ath*] *a* interlined with a caret after Hand 2 had blotted out the original letter following *e* 2400] folio number *(29.* above and to the right of this line

but yf he haue, & saie that he is sorrye,
It is a worse fault yf he be not trewlye.

Lamy: my lord such sorrow cannot be suspected,
heere, take yor honord wife, & Ioine yor hand*e*s.
I will be shee hath married you againe,
& gent, I do Invite you all
this night to take my house, where on the morrow
to heighten more the reconcileing feast,
Ile make my selfe a husband, & a guest. — *Exeunt.*

Actus Quintj: Scæna Prj

Enter: Montaigne: and Charlote

Char: well, now I am sure you are mine

Mont: I am sure I am glad.
I haue one to owne me then, youle finde me honest
as these dayes goe ynough, poore wthout question,
wch beggers hold a vertue, giue me meate, & I
shall do my worke, else knock my shooes of,
& turne me out againe.

Char: you are merry, fellow.

Mont: I haue no great cause.

Char: yes, my loue to ye.

Mont: that*e*s as wee make or game.

Char: why you repent then.

Mont: faith no. worse then I am I cannot bee,
much better I expect not, I shall loue you
& when you bid me goe to bed, obaye,
lye still. or moue, as you shall minister,
keepe a foure nobles nag, & a Iack *Merlin*
learne to loue Ale, & playe at too hand Irish
and theres the all I aime at. [Fol. 29b]

Char: nay sweet fellow, Ile make it something better.

Mont: yf you doe youle make me worse.
now I am poore and willing to doe well.

2439 [2]*a*] blotted

hould [me] me in that course, of all the kinges creatures
I hate his coyne, keepe me from that, & saue me,
for yf you chance out of yor huswiferie
to gleane a hunderd pound or too, bestowe it
in plumbe broathe, ere I knowe on't, elce I take it
I seeke out a hunderd men that wante this monye,
showre it among em, they cry noble *Montaigne*,
& so I stand agen at liuery

Char: you haue pretty fancies sir, but married once,
this charitye will fall home to yor selfe.

Mont: I would it would, I am afraide the loosenesse
is yet scarce stopt, thought it haue nought to worke on
but the meere ayre of what I haue had.

Char: prettye.

Mont: I wonder sweet heart why youle marry me,
I can see nothing in my selfe deserues it,
vnlesse the hansome wearing of a band,
for thates my stocke now, or a paire of garters
necessitye will not let me loose.

Char: I see sir a great deale more, a hansome man, a husband,
to make a right good woeman trulye happie

Mont: lord where are my eyes, either you are foolish.
as wenches once a yeare are, or far worse,
extreamely vertuous, can you loue a poore man
that relyes on cold meate, & cast stockinges.
one onely sute to his backe, wch now is mewing,
but what wilbe the next coate will pose *Tristram*,
if I shold leavie from my frendes a fortune
I could not raise ten groates to pay the preist now,

Char: Ile doe that dutye, tis not meanes, or monye.

t: Lamira: — makes me persue yor loue, were yor minde banqrout
I would never loue you,

Mont: peace wench, heres my ladye,

Lami: nay never shrincke ith wetting for my presence,
doe you finde hir willing *Montaigne*.

2447 *chance*] *h* altered

Mont: willing madame.

Lamira: how daintye you make of it, doe not I knowe
you two loue one another,

Mont: certaine madame I thinke ye aue revelations of these
matters. yor ladieship cannot tell me when I kist her,

Lamir: but she can sir

Mont: but she will not madame.
for when they talke once tis like ffairye monye, [FOL. 30a]
they get no more close kisses,

Lamira: thou art wanton,

Mont: heaven knowes I need not, yet I wolld be lustye,
but by my troth my provender scarce prickes me.

Lamira: It shall be mended, *Montaigne*, I am glad you are
growne so merrie

Mont: so am I to madame

Lami: you two will make a hansome consort.

Mont: yes madame yf my ffidle faile me not,

Lami: yor ffiddle, why yor ffidle, I warrant thou meanest
(madlye.

Mont: can you blame me, alas I am in loue.

Char: tis verie well sir

Lami: how longe haue you bin thus

Mont: how? thus in loue.

Lami: you are verie quick sir, no, I meane thus pleasant,

Mont: by my troth madame, ever since I was poore

Lami: a litle wealth would change you then.

Mont: yes ladye, into another sute, but never more
into another man, Ile bar that mainlye.
the wealth I get henceforward shalbe charm'd
for ever hurting me, Ile spend it fasting.
as I live noble ladye, there is nothing

2487] folio number *(30* above and to the right of this line

I haue found directlye cures the melancholye
but want and wedlocke, when I had store of monye.
I simperd sometyme, & spoke wonderous wise.
but never laught outright, now I am Emptye,
my heart soundes like a bell, & strikes a both sides.

Lami: you are finely temperd *Montaigne*

Mont: pardon ladye, yf any waie my free mirthe haue offended,
twas meant to please you, yf it proue to sawcie,
giue it a frowne & I am ever silenc'd.

Lami: I like it passing well, pray followe it.
this is my daye of choice, & shalbee yo^{res} too,
'twere pittye to delaye ye. call to the steward
& tell him tis my pleasure he should giue you
500 crownes, make yor selfe hansome *Montaigne*,
let none weare better clothes, tis for my credit,
but pray be merrie still,

Mont: yf I be not,
& make a foole of twice as many a hundred*es*,
clap me in canvas ladye. ——————— *Exeunt*.

Ent: Lauerdure: Lapoope: and Maly=corne

Lauerd: I am strangely glad I haue found the misterye
of this disguisd boy out, I ever trusted
It was a woeman, and how happelye [Fol. 30b]
I haue found it so, & for my selfe I am sure
one that wolld offer me a thousand pound now
(& that*es* a prettye som̄e to make one stagger),
in ready gold for this concealement, could not
buy my hope of hir, shees a daintye wench,
& such a one I finde I want extreamelye,
to bring me into credit, beautye does it

Maly: say wee all meich heere & stay the feast now,
what can the worst bee. wee haue playd the knaves
that*es* wthout question

Lapoop: true, & as I take it, this is the first truth
wee tolde this 7· yeares, & for anye thinge,

2537 *gold*] interlined with a caret.

I knowe may be the last, but grante wee are knaves,
both base & beastly knaves

Maly: say so then.

Lauer: well.

La poop: & likewise let it be considerd, wee haue wrongd
& most maliciouslye, this gent,
wee cast to staie with, what must wee expect now,

Maly: I, theres the pointe, wee wolld expect good eateing.

Lapoop: I knowe wee would, but wee maye finde good beateing.

Lauer: you saie true gent, & by my faith
though I loue meate as well as any man
I care not what he bee, yf hee eate a god*e*s name,
such crab sawce to my meate will turne my pallat,

Maly: theres all the hazard. for the frozen *Montaigne*,
has now got springe agen. & warmthe in him,
& wthout doubt, dares beate vs terriblye,
for not to [mynt] mince the matter, wee are cowardes,
& haue & shalbee beaten when men please
to call vs into cudgelling.

Lapoop: I feele wee are verie prone that waie

Lauer: the sonnes of *Adam*.

Lapoop: now heere then rest*e*s the state a'th question,
whether wee yeild our bodies for a dinner
to a sounde dog whip. (for I promise ye
yf men be giuen to correction,
wee can expect no lesse,) or quietlye
take a hard egge or too, & ten mile hence
baite in a ditch, this wee maye do securely.
for to staie here about will be all one
yf once o^{r} morrall mischeefes come in memorye.

Maly: but pray ye heere me, is not this the daye
the virgin ladye doth elect hir husband.

Lauer: the dinner is to that end.

2562 *mince*] interlined with a caret   2575 *in*] *n* blotted

Maly: verie well then, saie wee all staie, & saie wee scape this whiping, [FOL. 31a]
& be well Entertainde, & one of vs carrie the ladye

Lapoop: Tis a seemelye sayeing, I must confesse, but yf wee staie,
how fittly wee maye applye it to o^{r} selves (ith end)
will aske a christian feare. I cannot see
yf I saie true, what speciall ornament*e*s
of art or nature (lay aside o^{r} lyeing
whoreing & drinkeing, wch are no great vertues,
wee are Endewd wthall to win this ladye,

Maly: yet weomen goe not by the best part*e*s ever, that I haue
found directlye.

Lauer: why should wee feare then. they choose men
as they feede, sometime they settle
vpon a white broath face; a sweet smooth gallant,
& him they make an end of in a night.
sometimes a goose, sometimes a groser meate,
a rumpe of beefe, will serve em at some season,
& fill their bellyes too, though wthout doubt
they are great devourers, stocke fish is a dish
yf it be well drest, for the tufnes sake,
will make the prowdest of em longe & leape for't,
they'le ron mad for a pudding ere they'le starve,

Lapoop: for my owne parte I care not, come what can come,
yf I be whipt, why so be it, if cudgelld
I hope I shall outlive it, I am sure
tis not the hundreth tyme, I haue beene seru'd so,
& yet I thanke the *fates* I am here, too.

Maly: heres resolution

Lapoop: a litle patience & a rotten apple
cures twentye worse deseases, what saie you sir,

Lauer: marry I saie sir, yf I had beene aquainted
wth laming*e*s in my youth, as you haue beene,

2579] folio number (*31* above and to the right of this line written over erased *&*   2588 *weomen*] ^{1}*e* interlined with a caret   2592 ^{2}*a*]

wth whippinges and such benefites of nature
I shold do better, as I am Ile venture,
& yf it be my lucke to haue the ladye,
Ile vse my fortune modestly. yf beaten
you shall not here a word, one I am sure of,
& yf the worst fall, she shall be my phisique,

Lapoop: letes go then, & a merrie winde be wth vs.

Maly: Captaine, yor shooes are olde, pray put em of,
& let one flinge em after vs, be bold sirs,

Lauer: and how so ever our fortune falls, letes beare
an equall burden, yf there bee an od lash,
weele parte it afterwardes.

am arm'd at all pointes. ——— *Exeunt*

A Banquet: Set out: then Enter: Orleance: & his Ladye: Arme in Arme: Amience: Lamira: Charlott drest as A Bride: Montaigne: Veie braue. Longauile: Dubois: Lauerdure: Malycorne: Lapoop: & Attendantes: [Fol. 31b]

Lamira: seate yor selues noble lordes, & gent
you knowe yor places; many roial wellcomes
I giue yor grace, how louely shewes this change.
my house is honord in this reconcilement.

Orle: Thus madame, must you doe.
my lady now shall see you made a woeman,
& giue you some short lessons for yor voiage.
take hir Instructions ladye, she knowes much.

Lamira: this becomes you sir:

Lady: my lord must haue his will

Orle: tis all I can doe now sweet heart, faire ladye,
this to yor happie choise, brother *Amience*,
you are the man I meane it to,

2618–19] vertical rule in margin blotted

Amie: Ile pledge you.

Orle: & with my heart,

Amie: wth all my loue I take it

Lami: noble lordes,
I am prowde ye haue done this daye, so much content,
& me such estimation, that this houre
(in this poore house) to knit a league for ever,
for so I knowe ye meane it.

Amie: I doe ladye. |*: Orle:* |*:* & I my lord,:| *omnes:*|: ye haue done a worke of honor,

Amie: giue me the cup. where this health stoppes,
let that man be eather verie sicke, or verie simple,
or I am verie angrie. sir to you, —
madame, me thinks this gent might sit too,
he wolld become the best on's.

Orle: pray sit downe sir,
I knowe the ladye of the ffeast expectes not
this daye so much ould custome.

Lami: sit downe *Montaigne*. nay never blush for the matter,

Mont: noble madame, I haue too tyes against it, & I dare not,
duetye to you first, as you are my ladye,
& I yor poorest servant, next the custome of this dayes
(cerimonye

Lami: as you are my servant, I may cõmaund you then.

Mont: to my life lady.

Lami: sit downe, & here, Ile haue it so.

Lami: sit downe man, never refuse so faire a ladyes [pr]offer. [Fol. 32a]

Mont: It is yor pleasure madame, not my pride,
& I obey. Ile pledge ye now my lord, – *Monsir Longauile*,

Long: I thanke you sir

Mont: this to my ladye, & hir faire choise to day. & happinesse.

2667] folio number *3(2)* above and to the right of this line

Long: tis a faire health, Ile pledge you though I sinke for't.

Lami: *Montaigne* you are to modest. come, Ile ad
a litle more wine t'ee, 'twill make you merry.
this to the good I wish you.

Mont: honord ladye, I shall forget my selfe wth this great bountye.

Lami: you shall not sir, giue him some wine,

Amie: I sweare you are a worthie woeman, & that man
is blest can come nere such a ladye

Lami: such a blessing. wet weather washes of my lord.

Mont: at all, I will not goe a lip lesse, —

Orle: tis well cast sir.

Maly: yf *Montaigne*. get more wine wee are like to heare on't.

Lauer: I doe not like that siting there.

Maly: nor I, me thinks he looks like Iustice.

Lapoop: now haue I a kinde of grudging of a beateing on me, I feare
my hot fit.

Maly: drinke a pace, theres nothing alayes a cudgell like it,

Lami: *Montaigne*, now Ile put my choice to you,
whoe doe you hold in all this honord companye,
a husband fiting to Enioye thy ladye,
speake directlye

Mont: shall I speake madame.

Lami: *Montaigne* you shall

Mont: then as I haue a soule. Ile speake my conscience,
giue me more wine *in vino veritas*.
heere, to my selfe, & *Montaigne* haue a care,

Lami: speake to the cause,

Mont: yes madame, first Ile begin at the lower ende.

Lauer: haue at vs, | *:* [*Lapoop:* | : now for a psalme of mercye.]

Mont: you good *Monsir*, you that belye the noble name of courtier,
& thinke yor claime good heere, hold vp yor hande.
yor wor^{p}: is Endited heere for a vaine glorious foole.

2686 *beateing*] ^{1}*e* interlined with a caret   2700 *psalme*] *s* written over *h*

Lauer: oh sir;

Mont: for one whose wit,
lyes in a ten pounde wastcoate, yet not warme.
ye haue trauelld like a ffidler, to make faces,
& brought home nothing but a case of tooth pickes.
you wolld be married, & no lesss then ladye,
& of the best sorte can serve you, thou silke worme,
what hast thou in thee to deserue this woeman.
)e but the poorest peece of man, good manners,
theres nothing sound about thee, faith thou hast none, [Fol. 32b]
it lyes pawnd at thy silkemans, for so much lace
thy credit wth his wife cannot redeeme it,
thy cloathes are all the soule thou hast, for so
thou [ne] saue'st them hansome for the next great tiltinge,
(let who will take the tother, thou wert never christend
[a] vppon my conscience), but In barbers water,
thou art never out ath bason, thou art rotten,
& yf thou darest tell truth, thou willt confesse it.
to kill the noysomnesse of [.]ich, thy skin
lookes of a chess=nut cullor, greasd wth amber.
all woemen that on earth do dwell, thou louest,
yet none that vnderstand, loue thee agen,
but those that loue the spittle, get thee home
poore painted butterflye, thy sommers past,
goe sweat, & eate drye[d] mutton, thou maiest liue
to doe so well yet, a bruisd chambermaide
may fall vppon thee, & advance thy follyes,
you haue yor sentence, now it followes Captaine
I treate of you.

Lapoop: [pray god] I wish I may deserue it.

Mont: you are a rascall Captaine

Lapoop: a fine calling.

Mont: a water coward.

Amie: he wolld make a prettye stuffe.

2719 *vppon*] interlined with a caret *In*] written over erased letter 2733 *I wish*] interlined with a caret.

Mont: may I speake freelye madame,

Lami: heres none tyes you.

Mont: why shouldst thou dare come hether wth a thought
to finde a wife heere fit for thee, are all
thy single monye whores that feede on carrott*e*s,
& filld the highe grasse wth familiars,
falne of to footemen. prethee tell me truely,
for now I knowe thou darest not lye, couldst thou not
wishe thy selfe beaten well, wth all thy heart now,
& out of paine, saie that I broake a rib
or cut thy nose of, wert not mercifull for this ambition.

Lapoop: doe yor pleasure sir, beggers must be no choosers.

Orle: he longes for beateing.

Mont: but that I haue nobler thought*e*s possesse my soule,
then such browne bisket, such a peece of dog fish,
such a most maungie mackrell eater, as thou art,
that dares doe nothing that belong*e*s too'th *Sea*
but spue, & catch ratt*e*s, & feare men of warr
thoughe thou hast nothing in the world to loose
a boorde thee, but one peece of beefe, o⟨
wthout a cocke, for peace sake, & a pitch barrell, [Fol. 33a]
Ile tell thee, yf my time were not more pretious
then thus to loose it, I wolld so rattle thee
It may bee beate thee, & thy puefellow[,]
the marchant there of Eele skins, tell my wordes
or blowes or boeth, made ye too branded wretches,
to all the world, heere after. you wolld faine to
venter yor bills of ladeing for this ladye,
what wolld you giue now for hir, some five fraile
of rotten figg*e*s good godson. wolld you not sir.
& halfe a pinte of olives, & a parratt
that speakes highe dutch. can all thou ever saw'st
of thine owne fraught*e*s from *Sea*, or cosonage,
(at wch thou art as expert as the deuill),

2758] folio number *(3⟨3)* above and to the right of this line; folio number *33*, added in a modern hand interlined with a caret

2760 *so*]

nay sell thy soule for wealth to, as thou wilt doe,
forfaite thy frend*es*, & raise a mynt of monye,
make thee dreame all these double, could procure
one kisse from this good ladye, canst thou hope
she wolld lye wth such a nooke of hell as thou art,
& hatch yonge marchant=ffuries, oh ye dog bolt*es*,
that feare no god but *Dunkirkes*, I shall see you
serve in a lowsye lime boate, ere I dye
for walkinge cheese, & butter, billingsgate
wolld not Endure, or bring in Rotten pippins.
to cure blewe eyes, & sweare they came from *China*.

Lami: vex em no more, alas they shake

Mont: downe quickly a yor marrowe bones, & thanke this ladye.
I would not leave you thus else, there are blankett*es*
& such delight*es* for such knaves, but feare still,
'twill be revenge ynough, to keepe you wakeing,
ye haue no minde to marrie haue ye.

Lapoop: surely no great minde now.

Mont: nor you

Maly: nor I, I take it.

Mont: two Eager suitors.

Lauer: [troth] tis wonderous hott, god blesse vs from him.

Lami: you haue tould me *Montaigne*,
who are not fit to haue me, let me knowe
the man you would pointe for me.

Mont: there he sitt*es*. my lord of *Amience* madame[,] is my choice,
hees noble every waie, & worth a wife wth all the dowers of
(vertue.

Amie: doe you speake sir out of yor frendship to me,

Mont: yes my lord, & out of truth, for I could never fflatter.

⟨*Amie:*⟩ I will not saie how much I owe you for it,
⟩ that ⟨ ⟩ere but a promise, but Ile thinke ye
⟩de you in d⟨ ⟩e of f⟨
⟨ ⟩

2791 ^{2}*I*] ? added by Hand 2

Lami: my lord*e*s, I must confesse the choise this man hath made [FOL. 33b]
is everye waie a great one, yf not to greate,
& no waie to be slighted, yet because
wee loue to haue o^{r} owne eyes, sometimes in't,
giue me a little libertye to see
how I could fit my selfe yf I were put too't.

Amie: madame wee must.

Lami: are ye all agreed.

Omnes: [wee bee] *all laydy*

Lami: Then as I am a maide, I should choose, heere.
Montaigne, I must haue thee.

Mont: oh madame, I haue learnt to suffer more
then you can (out of pittye) mocke me wth, this waie especially.

Lami: thou thinkest I Ieast now,
but by the loue I beare thee, I will haue thee.

Mont: yf you could be so weake to loue a falne man,
he must deserue more then I ever can,
or ever shall (deere ladye) looke but this waye
vppon [this] that lord, & you will tell me then
your [.]eyes are no true choosers of good men,

Amie: do you loue him trulye ladye,

Lami: yes my lord, & will obaye him trulye, for Ile marrie him
& Iustlye thinke. hee that has so well seru'd me
with his obedience being borne to greatnesse
must vse me noblye of necessitye, when I shall serue him.

Amie: 'twere a deepe sinne to crosse ye, noble *Montaigne*,
I wish ye all content, & am as happie
in my frend*e*s good, as it were merely mine,

Mont: yor lordship does Ill to giue vp yor right,
I am not capable of this this great goodnesse,
there sit*e*s my wife that hold*e*s my trothe.

Char: Ile end all. I woode ye for my ladye, for her wonne ye,
& now giue vp my title, alas poore wench
my aimes are lower far.

2813 *all laydy*] Hand 2 2823 *that*] interlined with caret after *vppon*

Mont: howes this sweet heart.

Lami: sweet heart tis so, the drift was myne, to hide
my purpose tell it struck home.

Omnes: giue ye Ioye

Lami: prethee leave wondering, by this kisse, Ile haue thee,

Mont: then by this kisse, & this, Ile ever serue ye.

Long: this gent & I sir, must needes hope once more to follow
(ye.

Mont: as frend*es* & fellowes, never as servant*es* more.

ng: *Dubois:* you make vs hapie.

Orle: frend *Montaigne*, you haue taught me so much honor,
I haue found a fault in my selfe, but thus
Ile purge my conscience of it, the la⟨ ⟩l⟨
I tooke by falce playe fr⟨ ⟩ you, ⟨
contrition and Intirenesse of affection [Fol. 34a]
to this most happie daye. agen I render,
be m^{r} of yor owne, forget my malice,
& make me worthy of yor loue, lord *Montaigne*,

Mont: you haue wonne me, & honor to yor name,

Maly: since yor lordship has begun good deedes, weele follow.
good sir, forgiue vs, wee are now those men
feare you for goodnes sake, those somes of monye
vniustlye wee [detainde] detaine from you, on yor pardon
shall be restorde agen, & wee yor servant*es*

Lapoop: you are verie forward sir, it seemes you haue monye,
I pray you lay out, Ile pay you or praie for you,
as the *Sea* workes,

Lauer: their pennance sir Ile vndertake, so please ye
to grante me one concealement.

Long: still a begging

Mont: what is it sir

Lauer: a gentlewoeman.

2853] folio number ⟨*(34)*⟩ above and to the right of this line; folio number *34*, added in a modern hand

Mont: in my guift.

Lauer: yes sir in yores

Mont: why bring her forth & take hir. — *Exit Lauerdure.*

Lami: what wench wolld ye haue.

Mont: anye wench I thinke — ***Ent: Lauerdure: & Viram:***

Lauer: this is the gentlewoeman, ***as A woeman:***

Mont: this, tis my page sir,

Vira: no sir, I am a poore disguisd ladye
that like a page hath followed full long, for loue good [wot] sooth.

Omnes: a ladye.

Lauer: yes. tis a ladye

Mont: It may bee so; & yet wee haue laine together,
but by my troth I never found hir ladye

Lady Orle: why wore you boyes cloathes.

Vir: Ile tell you madame, I tooke example
by two or three playes, that me thought concearnd me
I tooke that habit, (madame

Mont: why made you not me aquainted wth 't,

Vir: Indeed sir I knew it not my selfe
vntell this gent opend my dull eyes.
& by perswasions made me see it

Amie: could his power in wordes make such a change

Vir: yes, as truly woeman as yor selfe my lord.

Lauer: why but harke you; [t]are not you a woeman then,

⟨*Vir:*⟩ yes. as much as you are, but since I am heere,
⟩midst so faire a presence, Ile open all.
⟩th is, ⟨ ⟩ am no other then that I seem'd
at first to bee, a boy, only as poore suspected [Fol. 34b]
Innocentes sometimes, to quit their vexed bodies
from the plague of tortors, by force'd paines
confesse those thinges they never did, so forced
was I to this exchange

2879 *sooth*] interlined with a caret

Lauer: I am gulld, I am gulld

Vir: for trust me gent, never did the ghost
of a deceased churle haunt the place where
hee had hid his gold wth more Insatiate greedines,
then this blinde conceited youth did me, no place
could free me from, tell at last I agreed
to say as hee would haue me, & by that meanes got
some rest, & now I dare be my selfe againe,

Mont: I'st ene so, how doe you like yor masculine ladye.

tet:

Lauer: so well, that yf it please you to change,
I shall be much thankefull.

tet: Lami: O keepe yor first choice.

Lauer: ha! crost in my first loue, I'me ene ashame'd of my

tet: Mont: come, chere vp, wee are all frend*e*s, I haue (selfe.
not receiud more wrong*e*s then I am willing to forgiue,
but you shall not hence vntell the marriage feast be
(past.

Amie: *Montaigne*, much Ioye attend thy marriage bed.
by thy example of true goodnes, *Envy* is exild,
& to all honest men, that truth Intend,
I wish good luck, faire *fate* be still thy frend.

——*Exeunt*

—*ffinis*/

Ihon

This Play. being an olde One
and the Originall Lost was
reallowd by mee. This: 8. febru.
1624
Att the Intreaty of Mr ⟨

2926 *Iohn*] Hand 3 2927–31] Hand 4 2930] *X Taylor*/ precedes this line